How to Do More with Less

YOUTH MINISTRY
on a Shoestring

Lars Rood

 ZONDERVAN®

 youth
specialties

ZONDERVAN.com/
AUTHORTRACKER
follow your favorite authors

ZONDERVAN

Youth Ministry on a Shoestring
Copyright © 2011 by Lars Rood

YS Youth Specialties is a trademark of YOUTHWORKS!, INCORPORATED
and is registered with the United States Patent and Trademark Office.

This title is also available as a Zondervan ebook.
Visit www.zondervan.com/ebooks.

Requests for information should be addressed to:

Zondervan, *Grand Rapids, Michigan 49530*

ISBN 978-0-310-67156-5

Cover design: LUCAS Art & Design
Cover photography: Masterfile
Interior design: Matthew Van Zomeren

Printed in the United States of America

11 12 13 14 15 16 17 18 /DCI/ 22 21 20 19 18 17 16 15 14 13 12 11 10 9 8 7 6 5 4 3 2 1

Contents

Introduction: The Shoestring Mindset 7

Part 1: **Stuff You Can Use
on a Shoestring Budget** 11

Chapter 1: What Is a Resource? 13

Chapter 2: Space 17

Chapter 3: Technology 25

Chapter 4: Money (How to Make It Stretch Further). . . 33

Chapter 5: Transportation/Vehicles 39

Chapter 6: Community/City Resources 47

Chapter 7: Dumpster Diving, Garage Sales,
Thrift Stores, Hardware Stores 51

Part 2: **People/Partnerships That Can
Bolster Your Shoestring Budget** 55

Chapter 8: Network 59

Chapter 9: The Congregation 65

Chapter 10: Friends and Family. 69

Chapter 11: Parachurch Ministries. 73

Chapter 12: Camps, Colleges, Seminaries 77

Chapter 13: Training Organizations 83

Chapter 14: Denominational Help 87

Chapter 15: Other Ministries in Your Church 89

Part 3: **Intangibles That Can Bolster Your Shoestring Budget** 93

Chapter 16: History 97

Chapter 17: Longevity/Relational Equity 103

Chapter 18: Failures/Successes 105

Chapter 19: Dreams and Aspirations 109

Chapter 20: Education. 113

Chapter 21: Pastoral/Church Leadership Support 117

Chapter 22: Community Support 121

Part 4: **Practical Planning on a Shoestring Budget** 123

Chapter 23: Lock-Ins on a Shoestring. 127

Chapter 24: Retreats/Camps on a Shoestring 133

Closing Thoughts 137
Other Shoestring Stories. .139

THIS IS MY FIRST BOOK. Hopefully it's not my last. I dedicate it to everyone who's put up with me for the last 20 years in youth ministry. From John Losey (who gave me my start at Forest Home and forced me to always think differently) and Mark Oestreicher (who gave me my first full-time youth ministry job and sent me to my second) to Roger Dermody (who believed in me and gave me opportunities to dream bigger than I had ever imagined).

And I thank all the youth ministry staff I've worked with, especially the interns and volunteers who really had to model what this book is about (because I never gave you any budgets of your own). I am a better youth pastor because of you, the amazing people God let me work with.

And to Danielle: You have lived this youth ministry life with me, and it hasn't always been easy. Thank you for always encouraging me.

The Shoestring Mindset

THE WORLDWIDE ECONOMIC RECESSION has had a ripple effect upon many industries, individuals, and organizations—not the least of which likely includes your youth ministry budget.

Many churches that had decent budgets in years past have felt the pinch, maybe for the first time in decades—and typically, their youth ministry budgets were the first to get cut. Youth ministries with small budgets have watched their resources diminish even more, and churches without any budgets at all are *still* without budgets. As a result, much of the belt tightening has affected our youth ministry programs as we've been forced to scale back programs, cut staff, stop providing scholarships for retreats and camps—and even cancel things completely.

This obviously isn't welcome news for those of us involved in the youth ministry world. We want to do camps, mission trips, service projects, overnighters, concerts, fun events, discipleship activities, games, and more. We want the ability to go where students are and occasionally have the resources to buy a pizza and some soda as a bonus for kids—simple things like that.

This book isn't aimed at figuring out how to generate more money so you can do more ministry; it's aimed at helping you think of ways that you can do more ministry with the resources already at your disposal—and even to do them for *less*.

The words in these pages aren't written for the purpose of giving you a list of things you can use and cheaper alternatives (although there will be quite a bit of that). The overall focus of this book is to encourage you to enter into all phases of ministry—planning, preparing, and even running events—asking the question, "Can we do this for less?" As you read this book I encourage you to consider thinking outside the box when it comes to resources.

Maybe you've been trying to do certain ministry activities that seem as though they should be "so simple" (and other churches seem to pull off with relative ease), but because you don't have the same resources other churches have, you consistently struggle. I want to help you take a look at every possible resource available to you and have you rethink your approach in terms of how you use them in ministry. You just may end up with a vastly different ministry because you took the time to answer, "Can we do this for less?" and then realized you possess resources all around you that you never tapped into before.

This book is divided into four sections: two pretty simple classifications, then one that's a bit more difficult to understand, followed by one section with some hands-on practical steps.

I call the first section **Stuff** because that's exactly what it focuses on. What "stuff" is around your church, community, and city that you could potentially use to do youth ministry?

The second section is **People/Partnerships**. I'm a network guy, and I love to partner with people. In this section you'll read a lot about not doing things alone and who could potentially help.

In the third section you'll read about things I call **Intangibles**—the things often hardest to explain but that often carry the most impact in terms of resources. You might find that, in reading this section, you're totally neglecting huge resources available to you.

Lastly there's a section called **Practical Planning** that shows you how I believe you could go about doing some shoestring planning. It includes examples that will help you draw conclusions about how to do youth ministry on a shoestring.

There are enough practical tips in each of these chapters for those of you who prefer to flip through books and skim, looking for tips. But the best way to read this book is to get to the end of each chapter and take some notes about the things each chapter discusses in relation to your own ministry. As ideas are presented to you, feel free to jot down how those ideas can be translated to your own ministry context so they can benefit your students.

The important thing to remember is that the "shoestring" approach, when all is said and done, is just an added step to all your planning that can allow you to do more for less. After you have something planned, take the time to add the step and evaluate all the ideas and programs by simply asking the question, "How can I shoestring this?" You might be amazed at how your subsequent ideas transform your original plans into something you didn't expect. You might be able to reach more students—even different students—do more creative ministry, and even do things better because you are doing it smarter.

I've asked some friends to share some of their tips, too, so look through the book for their sidebar testimonies about ways they've learned to save money while doing ministry over the years.

God's blessings on you as you embark on the adventure of doing youth ministry on a shoestring.

—*Lars Rood*

PART 1

Stuff You Can Use on a Shoestring Budget

chapter 1

What Is a Resource?

I'LL NEVER FORGET THE DAY someone handed me a $100,000 check for use in my youth ministry.

I thought I was the luckiest youth minister in the world! Now I'd be able to do everything I'd ever dreamed up! I was convinced that this money would literally make everything all better. I'd be running the best youth ministry with the most kids, and I'd be the best youth minister.

Take a couple of minutes to think about what you would do if someone handed you that kind of money. What types of resources would you buy? What trips or events or camps would you plan? Would you hire more staff? What youth ministry dreams do you have that an extra $100,000 would allow you to accomplish?

I had huge aspirations for how we would use the money. As you might expect, almost all the aspects of my dreams had something to do with "stuff" I thought our youth ministry needed. Therefore the first item to cross off my "stuff to do" list was remodeling our youth room. Our goal was to raise the roof, install new lighting and a new sound system, paint, and build a stage.

Of course we first had to redo the electrical circuitry because we wanted everything to look professional. That electrical work and new lighting ended up costing us about $35,000. And we still had to install the sound system and stage.

I used up half the money before I even had anything significant happen for the youth group. That reality caused me to begin thinking hard about what I could do for less.

After blowing through all the money in about six months, we did have a nicer youth room. We had a couple of safer vehicles to drive, and we had some great mission trips and camps that students were able to attend.

But we also raised an expectation among students (and their parents) that all camps and mission trips would be really cheap yet amazing. Unfortunately we couldn't live up to that unrealistic expectation the following year.

How We Define and Value Resources

One thing I've discovered after going through this for a while is that most youth workers tend to overemphasize the value of certain resources and not think enough about all the resources truly available to them—and for less or no money.

Our view of resources is pretty narrow. We tend to think about things in terms of the three "S words"—stuff, staff, and space. The belief seems to be that if we have a big-enough budget (i.e., the means to acquire more stuff) and a large-enough staff and a cool-enough space, then we'll have a great ministry. The problem with such a narrow view of resources is that we tend to get locked into that mindset—that those S-word resources (stuff, staff, space) are the most important, and as a result we're often pining away for more of those three resource categories—or perhaps considering moving on to youth ministry positions with more of those S-word resources.

What I've learned is that there are so many other areas to consider when thinking about resources. The smallest youth ministry with the tiniest budget, no dedicated youth space, and a part-time or volunteer youth worker can actually be better positioned for success because of the way that youth ministry looks at resources. Often smaller churches recognize their financial limitations and are more aware of other resources around them that they can use. In short, their mindset helps them think in ways that churches with bigger budgets, large youth staffs, and dedicated youth spaces might not see.

To that end, I'm simply defining *resources* within this book as "anything you can use for your youth ministry." This definition is incredibly broad—and that's the goal. Too often we get stuck in the mindset that the only resources that matter are stuff, staff, and space.

I'll be the first to admit that I'm not always very good at identifying resources. I often get focused on particular things and miss noticing great resources that are all around me. So I've gotten into the habit of taking time every couple of weeks just to think about what resources might be around that I can use. And as we dream, plan, and budget, I'm always asking myself, "What do we have and how can we use it in our youth ministry?"

The Truth about "Stuff"

The traditional youth ministry stereotype is that you need "stuff" in order to do ministry. I've struggled for years with this. I wonder, *Wouldn't it be great to have a closet full of things I can use to pull off anything?* I also imagine how it would be to have a huge warehouse full of stuff at my complete disposal, so that anytime I needed something I could rummage through it and find the perfect resource.

I've worked at two churches where I had pretty big selections of stuff just lying around. At one church I had everything necessary to pull off amazing houseboat trips—there were water skis, wakeboards, banana boats, life jackets, inflatable movie screens, hundreds of feet of extension cords, portable sound systems, fire pits, bumper buoys, spear guns, masks, snorkels, flippers, surfboards, tow ropes, etc. Because of all that stuff at my disposal, we pulled off some of the greatest houseboat trips you can imagine and created amazing memories for students in the process. (I hope they can look back and call those weeks the best weeks of their summers!)

But unfortunately, that's all they were. A week one year, another week the next year. The church spent thousands upon thousands of dollars for equipment that was used for just one week every summer— and then that stuff spent the rest of the year gathering dust in storage.

It's always refreshing to go to a church, walk into the youth room, and see immediately that the youth ministry is a serious priority. The youth room is filled with things that make it inviting to students, and from all appearances that youth ministry seems to have it all figured out.

Appearances, however, can be deceiving . . .

"Stuff" Doesn't Make a Youth Ministry

You can buy the most stuff and set it all up in the youth room—and have a really bad youth ministry. We often get caught up with feelings that we need all this stuff, or we can't do youth ministry. We get stuck in the mindset that the stuff at our disposal defines our ministries.

How many of us haven't wanted the new latest and greatest thing only to get it and not experience a better life? Worse yet, not experience the contentment, relief, or peace we hoped it would bring? This happens in youth ministry, too. If you get caught up in the bigger-and-better-stuff-is-needed-to-do-youth-ministry cycle, you'll never experience contentment, relief, or peace about your youth ministry.

So as you read through the remaining chapters in this first section, I want you to think through some specific "stuff" areas in your youth ministry and how you can find cheaper resources. I also want to encourage you to think within your own context not only about what resources you already have and may not have used in every way possible, but also about resources you've never thought about using.

These "stuff" chapters don't represent a definitive list. You won't finish this section and have a perfectly diagrammed map for your ministry that will make you impervious to budget changes. But there should be some tips from each chapter that will inspire you to consider options that can work for you and your youth ministry context. (And at the end of each chapter remember to take notes in the space provided, paying special attention to your own resources so you can start dreaming about how you can use them more effectively to do more fruitful youth ministry.)

chapter 2

Space

Traditional

Maybe you have a dedicated youth ministry room that's 100 percent set aside for your ministry. Your space may be a top-notch facility with all the bells and whistles—or maybe it's the run-down shack behind the church that no one wants to enter, so they decided years ago to give it to the youth ministry because "the kids won't care."

As I share in the previous chapter, I once spent a lot of (someone else's) money trying to create the best youth room possible to attract students; I failed to spend money wisely. Many of us get caught up in the belief that the "better" the youth room, the more effective the ministry.

Shoestring

Taking a look at youth ministry space from a shoestring approach will really change how and where you do youth ministry. In reality, I believe that the traditional youth room may, in fact, actually *hinder* ministry. Why? Because *it's all about students coming to you.*

The shoestring model, in contrast, often puts you in the students' world—in fact, the "church" goes *to* the students and the community. As a result, you don't need a great youth room if you take the time to think creatively about what spaces are all around that you can use on a regular basis. So put your shoestring goggles on and take a new look at some alternative spaces you could potentially use for your youth ministry.

Homes

Often students can get their friends to come to their houses easier than to the church. Are there homeowners among youth ministry families (or even church members at large) who would be willing to open their homes for events or activities? What about doing something like a "progressive dinner" at the homes of the elders or pastors of your church?

I sort of "fell into" realizing how great a resource this is. I was working at a church in Los Angeles when a new family joined our youth department. The mom was a big supporter of what we were doing, and she invited us to do our summer pool parties at their house. Before arriving at their house to check it out, I wasn't at all prepared for their amazing property. It was in Beverly Hills and used to be owned by a famous actor—in short, it was *huge*. The first night students showed up there, I knew we'd have no problems getting them to summer programs that year. They loved it.

Since then I've always made a point to consider whether some families in the church and in the youth ministry have homes well suited for youth group activities—much more than your traditional youth room. Of course there might not be a willing mansion-owner at your disposal for a resource, but I bet someone from the church owns a house with useful characteristics—even something as basic as a backyard with a hill where you could do all sorts of activities would be a great resource.

Coffee Shops

The trend lately has seemed to have been placing these in the lobbies of many of our churches, but at a lot of cost and, in my opinion, waste. Instead, why not just go build relationships at a coffee shop in a central location and host Bible studies and meetings there?

As I type these words, I'm sitting inside a big-chain coffee shop. I spend a lot of time here, and they know who I am. I run into a lot of parents, students, and church members here, too. It's nice to interact with them outside the church and in the community; plus, there are so many benefits to being at a coffee shop. First of all, I don't have to make coffee, bring snacks, or even make the room cool. Coffee shops already spend a lot of time and money doing that. Therefore I conduct many of my meetings here just because it's cooler than my space. (Make sure, though, that some coffee and snack purchasing is part of your meeting so the establishment doesn't feel used.)

Restaurants

Many restaurants have banquet rooms they'll let you use for free if you pay for food. Do your banquets off site in the community at a restaurant. Host meetings there. I did a senior guys' Bible study for an entire year at a Mexican restaurant near church. It was way easier to get guys to come there than to church! It's pretty funny in our community that every Wednesday morning the Chik-fil-A looks like it's been taken over by the neighborhood churches. It seems like everyone is hosting some sort of Bible study breakfast there. It's a perfect space really; students buy their own breakfasts, there's free Wi-Fi if you need it, and they generally really like us coming in there.

Colleges

Maybe there's a college or university near your church with great spaces you can borrow for free or rent for cheap. They often have gyms, theaters, pools, conference rooms, dorms, etc. Think about what kind of retreat you could do at a local college.

One thing we've done over the summer is stay at Christian colleges as part of our mission trips. Staying at their facilities is typically cheaper than hotel rooms and way more comfortable than sleeping on a church floor. The added benefit is that you can introduce students a little bit to the college experience—and using a Christian college's facilities better ensures that your kids won't be exposed to activities (e.g., partying) that'll worry you, their parents, and the church. You might even discuss a discount with the college for your stay since you're in many ways "advertising" the school to your students.

YMCA

Our local Y has a great outdoor pool and sports fields that we have the freedom to use. We have a partnership with the Y, as it uses our gym for a volleyball league, so we use their space when we need it.

Wilderness

One of the best retreats I ever put on was a prayer retreat in the local mountains. We hiked in, camped out, and spent two days praying, singing, and enjoying the nature all around us.

Growing up I was a part of a small church with no resources. But we did two camps every spring and summer: One was a bike trip and the other a hiking trip. Both were cheap and used the great outdoor spaces we had available to us for free.

I should point out that you may need to do some prep work before you simply cart your kids into the wilderness! I'm notoriously bad at packing. By *bad* I mean I'm a "minimalist," so to speak—which works for me but doesn't make teenagers very happy. For years I led trips to the Joshua Tree National Park in southern California and learned the hard way that just buying bagels, bananas, and water doesn't cut it as the "wow" breakfast for teenagers who want to eat a little more than that.

So before you utilize the wilderness and outdoor areas, make sure you know what items your kids will need and likely want. Guess how I learned to not stink at camping with teenagers? It's been a secret to this point, but I'll reveal it here: I asked some parents to go on a trip with us! That changed everything. Now that I'm about the age of those parents (i.e., my bones creak!), I realize how much I value comfort when I camp.

Another good place to check for outdoor resources is a camping/outdoor store like REI. You can also check out guidebooks at most libraries or find great free help online.

Camps

What camp facilities are available to you? Often they'll let you use their space if you just ask. Maybe you already have a relationship with a camp if you attend it for summer camp; they might let you use a meeting room for a one-day planning retreat over the winter—just ask! The worst they can say is no.

On a personal note, I'm just like many of you reading this book. I don't make a ton of money, and I have three kids of my own. So this year I contacted a big camp here in Texas and simply asked if they might be able to help me get them to summer camp. They were incredibly gracious and told me they love to help out youth workers who are spending their lives loving teenagers. I received great help from them just because I asked.

Malls/Stores

One of the great outreaches we do every year is Build a Bear Night, where we go to a local mall and put together bears that we take to a local hospital the following week. Youth groups have done many things in malls over the years from scavenger hunts to playing sardines. We often make sure we meet at the food court for a bite to eat before we're through. A mall possesses tons of options and is relatively cheap.

An important reminder: If you're not careful, you can also get into a lot of trouble with kids in a mall. I learned the hard way one year that the mall doesn't really appreciate 100 teenagers doing a scavenger hunt on a Friday night in the middle of the Christmas shopping season. Some malls are less of a wide-open resource space than they used to be because they've cracked down on a lot of group activities. So when in doubt, ask if it's okay.

Ranches

Maybe you live in an area where there are some wide open spaces owned by church or family members. We've done many retreats and camps at different ranches. They can be a lot of fun and are significantly cheaper than paying for campsites or other parks.

A note of caution: The word *ranch* can mean a lot of different things to different people. Here in Texas I've been offered the use of 100,000-acre properties with little or no services . . . not even toilets. That's a lot of space—and nowhere to go to the bathroom! Your youth group might not be impressed. In California where I lived for a long time, a "ranch" might be way smaller than that and have some pretty amazing amenities. Just ask what's available facilities-wise before you take your youth group anywhere for an extended period. You don't want to be surprised.

Hotel Ballrooms

Most hotels have great big rooms that are uniquely customizable. You could probably dream up something pretty great if you had that kind of space. A shout-out to Youth Specialties and the National Youth Workers Convention here: Every year YS takes over spaces in big convention hotels and does some pretty great stuff with them. Some of my favorite people—Mike King, Dan Kimball, and Lilly Lewin—take those spaces and create amazing sanctuary prayer and labyrinth areas every year.

The great thing about most hotel ballrooms is that they're set up to be flexible and change according to the needs of the groups who use them. When my wife and I got married, we hosted our reception at a hotel ballroom, and I'm pretty sure she thought it looked like something out of a fairy tale. We took a very simple space and—with drapery, lighting, and music—totally transformed the room. It's so easy with a little work to make hotel meeting spaces look amazing.

Movie Theaters

Besides renting space to show a movie, you could host a concert or a play, bring in a guest speaker, or hold an improv night. Here's some truth: I've never actually gone this route, but I've always wanted to. Maybe I don't think big enough, or maybe I just don't spend a lot of time in movie theaters, but I really like this idea.

When I was in college I attended a start-up church that met in a local theater. The space was ideal because it was near restaurants, coffee shops, and always had tons of parking. Plus it was well suited for activities. Even as I write this sentence I'm thinking about the theater that was just renovated only a few feet from where I'm sitting now—and all the cool things I could use it for my teenagers.

Other Churches

What if you partnered with another church and did something at their space? Doing a retreat that involves staying at another church is different and can be cheap—and it could be free if you agree to reciprocate with that church. Another church may have great spaces like a gym or a chapel or even a youth room—a big plus if you don't have such spaces at your own church.

My church has a pretty great facility, and we let people use it almost anytime they ask us. I love to hear their reactions when they show up because they're usually so stoked to see our space. My favorite thing about going to other churches is observing the cool things they're doing with their spaces, which percolates my own ideas.

The church I worked at in Los Angeles literally had a multimillion-dollar view from the youth room. A space like that was attractive not just for our own youth but also for other churches who came for prayer nights while looking down over the city lights.

Your Own Church's Facilities

Are there parts of your church that you haven't used before for your youth ministry? We use our sanctuary about once a year for a special event. We've got some pretty great hallways that we use for hallway tag. There are probably some areas that you've never before considered using that might turn out to be perfect for an event or activity.

Today I walked around the church with our pastor's son and asked him to give me his "tour" of all the parts of the church that he'd explored for the last 10 years. He took me to some spots that I didn't know existed and even showed me where the key's hidden to get on the roof of the church—which, by the way, sports a pretty amazing view of downtown Dallas. (Please don't tell my boss.)

Your Resources

Start writing here. *Space* is a pretty easy thing to think about. Write down every idea you can think of regarding how you can find and use the spaces at your disposal.

Stuff You Can Use on a Shoestring Budget

chapter 3

Technology

Traditional

I'll always remember when I bought my first Mac. The price tag was $3,000, and it had a really small monitor, a hard drive, and pretty much couldn't do anything except replace my typewriter.

Over the years I've acquired more fancy machines, software, and tech toys. I had the very first version of Final Cut Pro (video-editing software), which was really expensive at the time—and I never used it. We created great youth group Web sites and chat rooms. We've had fancy video-recording devices, cameras, and all kinds of TV and DVD players.

I pretty much had it all in the process of keeping pace with the world of tech. But unfortunately I didn't use any of those tools to their fullest potential, which meant that I wasted a lot of money.

Shoestring

The shoestring approach to technology is pretty simple: *Don't pay for anything!* With all the free applications and online services, I don't believe there's any reason to pay for tech stuff anymore. Even computers. (Yes, you read correctly!)

Fortunately there are plenty of folks out there who always want to possess the newest, fastest, and best-est machines out there—and all you have to do is convince those folks to give (or donate) their old toys to you and your youth ministry. The reality is that any machine less than three years old will meet the needs of a huge percentage of computer users. Even video and photo editing programs don't have to meet the standard of "newest" in order to work really well for the purposes of your youth ministry.

Last summer I traveled in Israel and then on the west coast of the U.S. for a month taking pictures and blogging every day, using only an iPhone. On the Israel trip in particular, parents and supporters of students back in Texas said they really felt as though they were on the trip, too. It's well within the realm of reality to do almost anything in the world of technology for free—or at least for very minimal expense. It's impossible to create a definitive list of shoestring ideas when it comes to technology, and all of us have different needs and uses for our particular ministries. My one word of advice is that when a piece of technology you want has a price associated with it, fire up Google and do some searching for free downloadable alternatives. Chances are good that someone has created a cheap or free version. Remember: It's easy to get locked into singular ways of doing things with technology. For example, I only use Apple computers, but Windows- or Linux-based machines are significantly cheaper. Personal preference will play into this a lot.

Google Docs versus Microsoft Office

Today my administrative assistant uploaded all of our youth ministry release forms—a huge number, by the way—to Google Docs. She did so to make things more streamlined. The online free functionality of Google Docs is just so much easier for us to use than Microsoft Office. Now, wherever I am in the world, if I need a release form I can log on to Google Docs, search for the student's name, and download or print the signed form. We try to use Google Docs collaboratively, too. For example, it's nice to upload documents there and give access to the docs to others who may need them. (Using the example again of a release form, we've given several lawyers access to them so they could work together on creating a new form for us.)

Facebook versus Web Page

Yes, my youth group has a Web page. Yes, no one ever visits it. Yes, we do almost everything on our Facebook Group page that we used to do through the Web page. I love Facebook, and our students especially love it. Just last week we had a random event come our way just because a Christian pro football player happened to be in town; one of my volunteers who knows him asked if he'd speak to our group. All I had to do was log on to our Facebook page, create an event invitation, and message everyone in our group about it. (And if you're so inclined, you could utilize any number of students who're adept on the Web and make them be in charge of your group's Facebook page.)

Twitter versus Text Messaging System

Okay, as of this book's publication, not all students are using Twitter, but their numbers are growing. And if they're not using Twitter, they can still "follow" a Twitter account that sends new text "tweets" to their phones. So our ministry is beginning to use Twitter more frequently.

One way we used it this year was with our youth basketball league. We have 300-plus boys in the league, so we created a Twitter account to message everyone about what games were being played on any given night.

iMovie versus Final Cut Pro

Like I noted earlier, I bought the very first version of Final Cut Pro for video editing, and I never used it. By *never* I mean to say that despite some effort on my part, I didn't successfully create anything with it. It was too far beyond my skill set. I'm a living, breathing example of why you shouldn't give a youth worker $1,500 to buy software unless you know that youth worker is tech smart—or has easy access to someone who is. I blew it and just went back to using iMovie, which is free. I soon became a movie-making genius. (Yes, I realize that iMovie doesn't have all the features of Final Cut Pro, and some of you may need or want the extra stuff on FCP, but shoestring ministry is all about getting more for less.)

iPhoto/GIMP versus Photoshop

Anytime people tell me they need to purchase Photoshop, I simply ask why. Nine times out of 10 the reason is because they believe it's the only avenue available to edit digital photographs. True, there are a select number of people who do need Photoshop—they're called "photographers" and "graphic designers," of which none of us reading these pages are (at least not full time, assuming youth ministry is our full-time gig). Therefore just about none of us need a tool like Photoshop.

Here's my advice: Skip the expensive programs and simply learn to get the most out of the cheaper or free alternatives. I've found that the little-brother program to Photoshop contains tools that help me do everything I need when it comes to photo editing. (And if it doesn't, I just ask those with more talent than me to use their expensive copies of Photoshop to do the projects. Now that's smart of me for once!)

Free Stock Images/Videos versus Clip-Art/Expensive Images

At some point you'll need access to quality stock images if you're creating anything visually oriented. But ask around, and you may find free images you can access before paying big bucks.

One really good idea that I learned a long time ago is to make certain to first ask your church graphic designer (if you have one) what resources he or she may have that you can use. Your graphic designer may have some old disks or even credits on sites that have fallen into disuse that you can take over. There are also a ton of free online sites where you can acquire stock images. I could list some here, but since they change all the time, I'll just say Google "free stock images" and see what you come up with.

iTunes for Podcasts versus Burning CDs/Streaming from Your Server

I've talked to a lot of hip, trendy churches that spend thousands of dollars creating systems to stream content live to the Internet. Streaming is getting cheaper, but it's still an expensive option. Most of us who desire to record and get our content on the Web are better off simply recording it, editing it, and then posting it.

One of my good friends, Tim Schmoyer, does this a lot with his weekly youth ministry radio show and his YouTube content. Not a lot of people listen to the "live" broadcasts but plenty subscribe to the content he posts to iTunes as podcasts.

I'm not super sharp when it comes to all things video and audio related, but there's one important truth I did learn a while ago: Some people in your youth ministry, church, or community *are* super sharp. Therefore ask them to help you. You might never understand them when they tell you at what bitrate to record your stuff, but they'll make you look and sound good. (Just nod when they talk and learn a few key words, and they'll think you're as tuned into tech as they are!)

Students' Cell Phone Video Cameras versus Purchasing Video Cameras

Last week a guest speaker shared with our group. At the last minute one of my leaders asked if we could videotape it. He ran into the office and grabbed a huge case containing the $3,000 video camera we bought five years ago when we were committing ourselves to make a bunch of great videos. He asked me for help, but I told him I didn't know how to use it and that he should just borrow a student's iPhone (with its high-definition camera) and record the event.

In the end the latter option is free, looks better, and is easier to edit and use. If you really feel like you need video cameras for ministry, just ask your church if someone can donate old ones to the youth group. You'd probably be surprised by how many you can obtain.

eMailing PDFs versus Printing and Snail Mailing Expensive Calendars

A couple of years ago I realized that snail mail is a really horrible use of our youth ministry resources. We were sending home calendars quarterly and also quite a few flyers and letters. What I realized was that in most cases students and families weren't sitting at home just waiting for the new youth ministry poster to show up in the mail. And as the post office continued to increase the cost of mailing items, we just couldn't afford it. So now in many cases we either just email documents as a PDF that recipients can print themselves if they want, or create the documents so that recipients can fill them out almost entirely digitally so that the youth ministry doesn't have to buy or use paper at all. We do still print a few things, but we're relying more and more on the digital world.

eMail Distribution Programs (e.g., MailChimp) versus Dedicated Database Programs

Okay, I'm going to step on a few churches' toes here. I'm guessing that if your church is like mine, you probably aren't in charge of your database. In fact your church may try to keep the youth ministry away from the database as much as possible. But it's also true in many cases that youth workers understand new tools more than the IT guy at your church who's still mad that you talked him into buying you an Apple product.

Many churches use unintuitive database programs that don't allow you to do a lot of super-helpful things. Fortunately my church is slowly embracing MailChimp, and I'm so happy about that. I actually care about the analytics side of email campaigns; I like to know what people click, when they open the messages, how long the messages sit in their inboxes before they're opened. I like to know how well we do when we target specific groups. MailChimp and other programs like it allow us to know those things. And in many cases they are free.

Students Are the Experts Now; Give Them Space to Create and Lead

This is true and will probably continue to be true. Many of your students probably know more about technology and resources than you do. In my own house I'm slowly becoming the second person to go to after my 10-year-old son is first consulted! He's on the technology team at school and really knows what to do in many situations. Using students' know-how is a great way to engage them. They're growing up in the digital world; unlike most of us, they know no other existence. Give them opportunities to use their skills.

Recruit People in Your Church to Teach and Train Students

This is probably one of the most underutilized shoestring resources. There are incredible experts in your church. You probably have some graphic designers, musicians, and other technologically skilled folks. Have you ever asked them to use those skills for your youth ministry? They might never want to go on a junior high retreat or lead a high school small group, but they might be willing to sit with students once a month and help them edit retreat videos or even just set up podcast resources for you. Maybe they could teach photo-editing classes or come on a service day and just take pictures. By all means, use their skills.

Your Resources

It might be most helpful if you begin by listing all the different uses you have for technology in your ministry and what your needs are . . . and try to mimic that list with "shoestring" ideas.

Technology

chapter 4

Money (How to Make It Stretch Further)

Traditional

In a typical youth ministry you have some sort of budget. It may be that you only have enough money to buy 20 pizzas for the whole year, or you may have a lot more cash than that. Typically when I plan my youth ministry events, camps, and activities, I put together a budget. I take whatever money is available and divide the number by how many students who attend to figure out the per-person price. Pretty standard way of doing things. Depending upon your church and community, however, this way of planning can severely limit the number of students who can attend events because many just don't have the money to cover the per-person price.

Shoestring

The whole key of this book is to do more for less, but there are some very specific ways of stretching dollars that I will try to list here. Here's a quick way to look at this: Some things cost a lot of money and have a big reward (e.g., a summer camp or a mission trip). Some things don't cost a ton of cash and also have big rewards because the relational time with the students is lengthy. But since it's easier to get big things paid for than the little things, one shoestring idea is to add a few extra bucks to the cost of the big things so that money is available to pay for the little things. For example, charge an extra $20 for summer camp per student, and you have a good chunk of your lock-in funded for the fall.

Coupon Books

For years I've kept an "entertainment" coupon book in my car. The buy-one-get-one-free lunches and the like are great. These books pay for themselves usually after you use it just a few times. I try to go only to restaurants listed in the coupon book for lunch meetings and date nights. As an added bonus I found a bunch of new restaurants that I probably wouldn't have discovered otherwise. Above all, these books can really stretch your youth ministry budget. I've used coupon books for bigger things as well, such as discounts for hotel rooms, rental cars, and even random things such as haircuts, picture framing, and once even for a bounce-house rental.

Craigslist/eBay

Don't buy retail or new when used is cheaper and acceptable. I'm sort of an online auction guru. I've sold three cars, tons of electronics, and also purchased many things online. My wife has literally decorated our house from Craigslist purchases.

Here's a funny example: One morning a few years back I saw a Mac computer for sale on Craigslist for $50 (realizing it was worth way more than that). At 10 a.m. I bought it, brought it home, and updated the operating system. At 10:45 a.m. I reposted it on Craigslist for $350 and sold it at 2 p.m. That same day I found a whitewater kayak on Craigslist for $250. So using my $300 profit from my computer "flip" I bought the kayak. My final score? How about $50 in my pocket and a "free" Kayak in my garage! All because I spent a little time just looking at stuff through online auctions.

You'll be surprised by how much available stuff there is, often at really great prices. My recommendation is that before you pay retail for anything you always look first to see if you can get something from a private seller. The reason I like Craigslist more than eBay is that there are no seller fees associated with Craigslist. The only issue is that you don't get a lot of buyer protection with Craigslist. But still, check it out; you'll be happy you did.

Online Coupons

There are so many sites now dedicated to coupons. Before I do anything I always do a quick Google search to see if there are any discounts. Recently we went on spring break and were planning on visiting some of the natural wonders in Texas. I did some research before we departed and found a few sites with printable coupons that I just stuck in my backpack. I ended up saving about $25 off admission prices. My advice is to never go to a store without already checking prices online and looking for coupons.

Thrift Stores/Garage Sales

Often people will give you discounts or let you go through first if they know you are with a church. Garage sales are often a huge bounty of youth ministry resources. What I like about them is that you can see and touch the merchandise. That tactile experience sometimes helps me to dream bigger and get more creative about stuff. Of course with most sales it's helpful to get there early because the best stuff disappears quickly. Another thing working in your favor is that most people who hold garage sales have only one purpose—to get rid of stuff. Sellers are often willing to bargain. And if you get there late and miss the best stuff, another advantage is that you can sometimes pick up sweet stuff really cheap. Thrift stores have great deals, too. Our local thrift store chain offers pretty significant discounts for joining their store club card program. I'm a huge fan of wandering around thrift stores and buying random stuff that we can use for ministry. Costume closets and random ugly furniture pieces can actually be cool additions to your youth room.

Rewards Cards

I love taking students to establishments that "punch" a card every time you get a sandwich or a burrito. I can typically get a whole card punched just from one or two visits with students. Most of my students are under the false impression that I'm just being nice going to the back of the line, but little do they know that when they don't get a punch on their card I take advantage of that and my food is often free. This works in a lot of coffee shops, too. Grocery stores and other chain stores do things like this as well. I once bought outdoor gear worth a few thousand dollars for the church (we had money then), and I received a pretty big dividend check back from the store at the end of the year which I was able to use to buy more things for the church.

Ask for Free Stuff

Stores often give stuff away. This is a great way to get your budget to last longer. So before you just pay for things, ask for them. You'll find that a lot of stores will do it. Here's a bit of advice in this area: You probably have some parents or adults in your church with connections—and who are also probably good at asking for things. So keep a few of these adults in your contact list and have them do some of the asking for you.

Don't Pay for Stuff You Can Get for Free

I pretty much say this everywhere in this book. So, yes, saying it again here is redundant, but you need to hear it again. Always think about what you can get for your ministry for less—and better yet, for free.

Delivery Is Always More
Expensive Than Takeout

Most people don't think about this, but picking up pizza from the restaurant is always cheaper than having it delivered to you. No, it's not as convenient, but shoestring thinking isn't always easier—it's just cheaper. A pizza place near us makes $5 pizzas. If we had them delivered, they would cost $7.50—plus we'd always feel obligated to pay a tip (not that there's anything wrong with tipping—it's just not very shoestring-y).

Making Food at Home Is Cheaper
Than Eating at Restaurants

Every other week I host a dinner at my house for our senior class. It's a pretty big group and ordering food can be expensive. It costs me about 60 percent less to make dinner at home for them than it does to order out. It's not as convenient and takes me a lot of time, but I decided to embrace it, and it's become something I value. I love dreaming up new recipes and ideas for Sunday nights, and the students actually see how much of a big deal I make out of putting together their food.

If you don't possess culinary skills, you could simply ask some parents or other leaders to take on that role. As a side note, this is a great way to get volunteers who're a little nervous around students. At my church we have a college ministry that operates a similar Sunday-night dinner. Four volunteers in that ministry have been cooking food for college students for almost as long as I've been alive! It became their niche, and they love it. (And it saves us lots of money.)

Beg or Borrow

Take note: People will give you things! So I've recently begun asking for things more often. I'm not sure why this is an area that's been hard for me, but it has been. But since our budget has been cut, I've become more open to it. I shouldn't be surprised by the results—they almost always say yes. One particularly great thing is the "borrow" option. In my community there are people who possess lots of "things" yet don't use them very much. So we're not opposed to asking to borrow cars, lake houses, ranch stuff, cameras, barbeques, etc. The worst they can say is "no."

Buy in Bulk to Save Big Bucks

Split the cost/use with others if you don't need it all or all the time. It's likely that none of us has an immediate need for 200 rolls of toilet paper unless you have a serious, uh, problem or are planning on TP'ing an entire city block. But all of us will likely use 200 rolls of toilet paper over the next three years. So if you have the space to store them, you can save a lot of money buying them in bulk.

Bulk buying was the only way to manage my summer youth group houseboat trips. And one of those purchases turned out to be my funniest ever: a truck full of bottled water. We took 150 people on the houseboat, and the temperature was supposed to hit 120 degrees each day. So I bought 50 five-gallon bottles of water. A really big hassle and amazingly difficult to move all that water around, but I saved us a ton of money on the trip.

Denominational Help

If you're under the authority of a denomination, ask it for scholarships or grants. Even in the midst of a recession and with budgets being cut, there are often accounts still designated for specific things. Maybe your denomination has cut a program but still has some of the funding for it—perhaps it will give you the money you need if you partner with a few other churches to do something. If you aren't part of a denomination, don't worry—there are still organizations that can help you. Another shout-out to Youth Specialties who recently helped me award scholarships to some local youth workers who couldn't afford to attend the National Youth Workers Convention! YS had that financial resource available, and I just asked for their help. They aren't a denomination, but you get my point.

Your Resources

In this section you need to start by listing any resources at your church you can use to make events or activities cheaper to put on. This is a broad category covered by many others, so think specifically about money here as well as coupons and reduced-cost retailers and things like that. And you never know—maybe someone at your church would be willing to buy you a coupon book.

chapter 5

Transportation/ Vehicles

Traditional

There are a couple of traditional models regarding vehicles:

Model #1

The church owns a couple of vans, some shuttle buses, or maybe even a full-size bus. This is an expensive model because the church has to license, insure, maintain, and clean the vehicles (and make sure drivers are trained). And as the youth worker, you'll probably catch all the blame anytime something goes wrong related to using the vehicles or if they're found dirty by any non-youth ministry driver. (Of course, chances are good that you'll deserve that blame!)

Model #2

The church owns no vehicles, so every time you need to get students somewhere, you rent buses (charter or school) or vans. There are a lot more regular costs associated with owning the vehicles, but you'll generally pay quite a bit by renting them, too. Insurance costs can also be pretty expensive if you pay the rental company's insurance to avoid using your personal insurance.

Shoestring

This approach does not compromise safety. Back in the day the cheap way of getting a bunch of students from one place to another was to just stack them like firewood in a 15-passenger van and sing funny songs 'til you arrived at the destination—even sardine-like travel was part of the youth group adventure. This is not that approach. The shoestring approach to saving money on transportation costs means you'll probably have a higher inconvenience factor. It's nice to have vehicles parked right outside the youth room, but that's the most costly way. The following are some shoestring ideas:

Eliminate Transportation Needs by Having Students Dropped Off/Picked Up at Predetermined Locations

I don't know why it took me so long to figure out this simple principle that solves all transportation issues. One thing to remember, though: Don't leave before everyone is picked up! Parents are busy, and sometimes (like you and me) they forget things. You don't want to get a phone call an hour later from a student who's still sitting at the place you left him. As you can guess, parents don't appreciate that very much.

Ask Parents to Drive

This does two things for you: First, it gets parents more involved in the youth ministry; and second, they incur the cost of gas—a key way to save on costs. Parents, also, likely own bigger cars (often SUVs and even vans) than your youth staff. And most parents are used to playing chauffeur for their kids, so they would probably be willing to drive.

Quick tip: If parents are driving to an event for you, invite them to be part of the event or do something cool for them, like giving them gift cards and then sending them to lunch or dinner while the event is taking place (and then have them come back when you need them for the drive home). This will help them want to keep helping you—and it's way cheaper to spring for a few gift cards than to rent a bus.

Ask Members of a Sunday School Class or Adult Class If They Can Sponsor an Event and Provide Transportation

This is an area we are just now exploring at my church. Quite a few Sunday school classes are always looking for ways to serve. What if their service project for a month was to provide transportation for a student event? (It would be even cooler if they came up with a visual theme so that all the drivers wear costumes and/or decorate their vehicles. That gives them something cool to do and doesn't cost you anything.) All you have to do is ask.

Borrow Vehicles from Another Church (Partner with Them)

When I was a youth pastor in Los Angeles, I worked at a church that owned a bus—and we often partnered with other churches with transportation limitations. So for example, I covered the cost of transportation and drove the bus (yeah, perhaps not a good idea!), and the other church covered food or something else. This was a big win for both youth groups . . . and I never crashed the bus once.

Rent from the School District

This may not work in your town, but I've been in towns before where the school district rented buses—with drivers—for significantly less money than what it would have cost to rent a tour bus. Plus, you'll probably need to get a large group somewhere at some point—and cars aren't the best option for big groups. I've done the school-bus-rental deal, and it cost me at least half of what a nice fancy bus would have cost. (And the students didn't complain too much.)

Ask People in Church If They'll Lend You Their Larger Vehicles

I've done this, too—and it works. Sometimes you just have to ask for help. What I've done is send an email to the congregation and let them know we need some vans for an event. Sometimes they come with drivers, and other times we've just had the access to the vehicle itself. If you go this route, take care of the cars! It might even be worth the $10 to get it washed afterward just to show how much you appreciate it. (Yes, a few washes cost money—but it's still way cheaper than renting a bus, and you're making a wise investment by being thoughtful—those folks might just let you borrow their vehicles again!) Oh, and this goes without saying, but I'll say it anyway: Don't crash a car you borrow. I won't confirm or deny that this has ever happened to me.

Ask a Local Business to Donate a Vehicle to Your Youth Ministry

Often local businesses have trucks, trailers, vans, etc., that they might be willing to let you use. Sure there are liability issues and all that, but it can't hurt to ask. You might be surprised by how many business folk associated with your church have vehicles they'd love to bless you with!

Ask Nearby Camps If They Can Provide Transportation

I say this in other places in this book, and I'll say it again here: *Camps need you more than you need them!* That may sound harsh, but what I really mean is that most camps exist to support the local church. I've had great relationships with camp officials who were always willing to help our youth ministry when we needed it. And all camps own vans. So why not ask a camp to come and be a part of your trip or event? Give them the opportunity to make a pitch to students and parents about coming to their camp, and then have them drive students to the event. Sometimes they already have relationships with some students, and having them drive to an event gives them the opportunity to reconnect with them—a win-win scenario.

Partner with Local Colleges and Rent Their Vehicles

This may be easier if you live near a local Christian college, but it's not out of the realm of possibility that any college might rent you vehicles. With the recession many schools are looking for additional revenue streams. Find the right person to talk to and be creative. They've probably never considered this, but if you explain it the right way, they may get fully on board and be willing to help.

Have a Team of Adults "Shuttle" Students in Fewer Vehicles

If your destination isn't too far away, create a shuttle service with just a few vehicles. One thing we did to make this work really well was having an event that occurred sort of simultaneously at two locations. That way we didn't have a group of students just sitting bored at one place waiting to get picked up while the other group was having a good time. Instead both locations had stuff to do, and we shuttled students between the locations with 10 vehicles.

Split Costs with Another Ministry at Church That Might Need Vehicles at the Same Time You Need Them

I did this one year with a truck we had to rent for an event. The rental car company charged us for a five-day rental, but I needed it only for two days. So I talked someone into carting everything to camp in the truck and using the truck for another project for the church. The other church group actually paid for 75 percent of the rental since their drivers used it more—but I got exactly what I needed out of the rental . . . and without paying full fare. This was a huge win for us. You can go this route with any kind of rental scenario, not just with vehicles. (Important tip: Make certain that it's legal for multiple people to drive the vehicle.)

Share Transportation Costs of Heading to Camp with Another Youth Group

I mentioned this previously, but we used to give lifts in our bus to other church's youth groups heading to camp. I provided the bus, drove it, and just asked the other youth group to pay for the gas. Since my church already owned the bus and I was the driver, our transportation costs went down to zero. You can do this with charter buses, too. Instead of incurring all the costs yourself, if you have the space, rent it with another church and split the costs. Of course to do this you'll have to build some relationships with other churches. If you don't have those relationships already, just call the camp and ask them to help you set it up.

Trade Your Car for the Weekend with Someone Else Who Owns a Bigger Vehicle

My youth staff members have really small cars—not very useful for getting anyone to camp. What we've done, however, is ask parents of our students if we can trade vehicles with them for a weekend. Funny enough some parents actually really enjoy getting to drive something smaller than their SUV or minivan for a weekend. It makes them feel younger and freer—maybe even "racy." (Well, maybe not!) Again make sure you give them clean cars filled with gas.

Find a Vehicle Rental Company That Offers Better Deals to Churches

This one requires some effort on your part to add a personal touch. I had a great relationship with a rental car company, and the people there would always charge me for the cheapest car they had available—then upgrade me to the vehicle I actually needed. Not too shabby! I also met with a rental car manager once and made an agreement that we'd rent from his company exclusively if he gave us the best deals. We had that arrangement for three years, and it worked perfectly. It was simple for me to just call ahead and tell them what I wanted. I didn't have to comparison shop or do any other research. I knew I was getting the cheapest rate. They almost always upgraded us from a lower-priced rental vehicle as well.

Use the Internet to Comparison Shop for Transportation

The Internet has made my "doing more for less" mantra a lot easier. Comparison shopping for transportation is really simple via the Web. I'd go so far as to say this is probably the area in which I'm most gifted. We look all over the place to find the best deals, and nine times out of 10 I end up saving a lot of money. It can take a lot of work to figure out how to do this, but after you get into a good rhythm of search processes and strategies, you'll do well.

Use Multiple Travel Agencies and Online Sites to Book Airfare

It's a competitive world in the travel market—so never feel as though you're locked into one travel agent or online site. In fact, I work them against each other! Don't get me wrong: I'm always honest and tell them I'm getting a quote from them and from other sources so they know up front that I'll almost definitely go with the lowest quoted price. Just to be clear: Sometimes the lowest price isn't the best deal.

With all the added fees that airlines are building into fares, you have to be very careful when you add up the total cost.

Group Travel Isn't Always the Cheapest Option

It just lets you book tickets without providing names. Therefore do sign-ups earlier and book airfare with student names and you can often get a cheaper price. It's less convenient because you have to know much earlier who's going on the trip, but it sometimes gives you a much better deal.

One summer I booked a bunch of airplane tickets and then worried that I wouldn't get all the spots filled. So we closed sign-ups really early, and I gave back the tickets I didn't need (which is possible with group travel). We still had some late sign-ups, but those families booked their own airfare for the trip. Most of those who booked their own airfare used frequent flyer miles or other travel deals to get cheaper airfares, which ended up saving them money and making their trip cost less, too.

Negotiate with Airlines to Waive Baggage Fees or Fly Airlines That Don't Charge Baggage Fees

Airlines are hurting and want your business—i.e., your money. To meet that goal, they've added a ton of confusing fees. Sometimes a simple phone call with the right customer service person can save you a lot of money. We booked flights on an overseas trip one summer but had to fly to New York City first. The airline wanted to charge us baggage fees for that portion. So I called and negotiated and got them to waive that fee. You never know until you ask. (We fly Southwest Airlines with our youth ministry every chance we get since they don't charge baggage fees.)

Your Resources

What transportation options do you have available to you? Write them all down.

_____

_____

_____

chapter 6

Community/ City Resources

Traditional

The traditional way of looking at community and city resources is to not consider them at all. Most of us don't spend a lot of time interacting with our cities to see what resources they have besides the parks that we show up at to play softball or have cookouts. It may be that you have some good resources in your city that you aren't taking advantage of.

Shoestring

Chances are good that your city has things (or people) you can use—parks, pools, hiking trails, gyms, theaters, fire stations, police officers, lifeguards, etc. In many cases these things are available to you and your youth ministry because they are public services in the town where your church is located. Many times they will be free or carry a minimal cost.

Gyms and Pools

We do a once-a-summer big pool party at the local pool. It costs $5 per student but it's a huge pool and we have 3 lifeguards, which makes it worth it. If your church doesn't have a gym and your community does maybe you can rent it for a fun night.

Parks

We host a big event called the "Fiasco Cup" every year. We pay a deposit and have the whole park to run our big messy event.

Trails

Lots can be done outside with students, both for fun as well as doing teamwork-building things or even spiritual pilgrimages or night hiking.

Fire Stations

Every year the fire department brings a truck over to our big Fiasco Cup and we use it to wash shaving cream off of kids.

Police Officers

We just took an off-duty police officer on our winter high school ski retreat. This was a huge win for us, as it helped maintain a good relationship with the police department—very valuable when other issues come up.

Lifeguards

You might be able to hire a lifeguard for a private pool swim for less money than paying for all the students to go to a public pool.

Theater

Maybe your city has a theater or performing arts center that you can use for an evening.

Civic Groups

Often there will be groups or clubs in particular neighborhoods that want to volunteer or serve your ministry.

Boy Scouts/Girl Scouts

These organizations often partner with churches and have service projects they regularly need to do. This is a great way to partner with the troop to get things built or fixed around the church.

Your Resources

This will depend a lot on the type of community you live in. Some communities have more resources than others. Write out some of the resources that you think would be available to you and then start doing some more research.

Community/City Resources

_____

_____

_____

_____

_____

_____

_____

_____

_____

_____

_____

_____

_____

_____

chapter 7

Dumpster Diving, Garage Sales, Thrift Stores, Hardware Stores

Traditional

There's not much here that fits in the category of traditional youth ministry—except maybe the "donate a cruddy couch to the youth group" deal that's been going on forever.

Shoestring

This is probably one of my favorite shoestring areas because it involves the most exploration, imagination, and ingenuity. Plus, this is the part of the shoestring model that costs the least yet often generates the best results. In this area you literally look for stuff that everyone else has discarded, or you build what you need from a bunch of parts. If you're not particularly gifted in this area, you might need to recruit others to help. For instance, I'm not particularly adept at buying stuff from a hardware store and building masterpieces out of them—but I've got others around me who think this way. One friend in particular is just fun to go to Home Depot with because when I walk down the aisles with him, I can see the wheels spinning as he's already designing something. My advice in this area is to not write off *anything*. You don't want to continually fill closets with junk without ever using it, but you do want to regularly schedule time where you can dream while wandering around these places.

Dumpster Diving

Sounds illegal at worst; gross at best. But it doesn't have to be. Businesses often throw away a ton of stuff that you might be able to use. You can simply call them up and find out if they have things that they're throwing away—they may just give them to you. There are always a few good spots to check out, too, that throw away some great stuff. We grabbed tons of refrigerator boxes over the years from the backs of appliance stores. You can do a ton of really creative things with boxes.

Congregation and Families

Let people know that you'd like to be contacted if anyone is throwing away anything that could potentially be useful for youth ministry. You may want to create a postcard saying that if they have any particular items (list them), they should give the youth ministry a call, and you'll pick them up.

Nonprofit/Church Donations

Lots of people like to give stuff to nonprofits. Check to see how this works for your church, but you might be surprised at the reaction. Folks have given us some pretty amazing things over the years. Some we keep. Some we sell.

Thrift Stores

I covered these places previously, but I'll add here that you should get into the habit of heading to a thrift store at least once a month and just wandering around. Of course you'll find the typical used couches from the 1970s that you (probably) don't want—but what about the old clothes or "big clothes" you can use for skit costumes? Thrift stores always have great stuff you may be able to use.

Garage Sales

Again, covered previously, but I'll add here that you may be able to talk people who're throwing the garage sales into giving your youth ministry the first look at what they are selling. They might even be willing to discount or just give stuff to you. After all, you're from a nonprofit organization—with your cooperation, they can write off their donations. Since people hold garage sales primarily to de-clutter their lives as opposed to earn extra money, you might prove a huge help in that pursuit. (Important Note: Above all, be courteous and thoughtful. If you have a truck or church van at your disposal, you might offer to help move some of their big stuff to your neck of the woods.)

Hardware Stores

I like the big box hardware stores. You can generally build things way cheaper than you can buy them. So pick up an "ideas book" and wander around and see what you can build. Nothing like aisles of PVC pipe, spray paint, bungee cords, and Christmas lights to have all the makings of a pretty cool Christmas display to put on your senior pastors' lawns. (No, they don't know about it!)

Craigslist

I try to make sure to check the "free" section pretty regularly. You'd be amazed at what kind of stuff people are trying to get rid of that to them might be junk—but to us in youth ministry might be treasure. (See my Mac and kayak story on page 34.)

Your Resources

You've got some homework to do in this area. My advice is to check out some of the local thrift stores. Get to know people there. Maybe they'll call you if they get something they think you might need. Scan when garage sales are happening and make a general announcement at church that you'd like people to call you when they're getting ready to discard their stuff.

Stuff You Can Use on a Shoestring Budget

PART 2

People/Partnerships
That Can Bolster Your
Shoestring
Budget

WHEN I STARTED OUT in youth ministry, my day went something like this:

1. Arrive at church office around 9 a.m.
2. Sit at my desk.
3. Wonder what to do for a few hours.
4. Decide to work on a calendar; cut out clip-art; try to be creative. (Yes, I was a rookie youth worker during the clip-art era!)
5. Work on some music for Wednesday night Bible study (the songs can't contain anything other than G, C, or D chords).
6. Think about Sunday message.
7. Do long-range planning.
8. Head to local school for sporting event; walk the campus alone; feel really awkward; say hi to a few kids.
9. Go home for the night.
10. Repeat steps 1 through 9 the next day.

What I modeled in my earlier years was pretty much the art of doing youth ministry alone, all the time, with nothing more than my own pretty weak gifts, skills, and talents. I had volunteers, but they just hung out with kids and didn't do much else; the only other paid staff worked in the copy room part time and generally wasn't very available to me.

Somewhere along the line a switch flipped in my head and I got incredibly dissatisfied with doing ministry alone. Then I began to realize that there were a whole bunch of people just like me in my town who loved teenagers and were actually really fun to be around. So I started inviting them to lunch. Then somewhere along the way they became my friends. Then as things happened in our friendships, we started to appreciate each other's gifts and talents and began realizing that because of our unique gifts we could offer each other reciprocal help.

Suddenly I wasn't alone anymore and knew I never wanted to go back to being the guy who just sat in his office wondering what to do every day. Now when I struggled to figure out things, I could call other youth workers and find out what they were doing—which greatly inspired me. As I got more comfortable networking, I made friends with people outside the youth ministry world—coaches, teachers, and parachurch ministry staff members (e.g., Young Life). I got to know people who worked at the YMCA and was even on a first-name basis with the baristas at the local coffee shop.

If there's one thing I'd tell anyone feeling unresourced in youth ministry, it's to make friends with people and learn how to partner and share resources. The example I always offer when talking about networking is how my neighbor and I each own lawn mowers. We use our lawn mowers only about 40 times a year each, but we both take care of them, and they each take up space in our garages. How much better would it be if we'd just partner and share one lawn mower?

I don't work for the National Network of Youth Ministries, but I'm friends with many of them, and I love their slogan: "Better Together."

Maybe you don't have all the people/partnerships available to you that I'll discuss in the next few chapters, but I encourage you to read about them all anyway—because you might be surprised as you brainstorm at the end of each chapter that you actually *do* have more resources than you originally thought.

So my advice is to think way outside your box in this area. I believe you'll find that even the most random people and organizations around—that seem to have absolutely nothing to do with youth ministry—might end up being your greatest resource.

chapter 8

Network

The Shoestring Benefits

Joining a youth ministry network might actually be the simple answer to how to make all things better for you in your ministry. Yes, I realize that's a pretty broad statement, but it's something I've seen repeatedly to be true.

In Dallas where I live there's a pretty amazing youth ministry network. There are regional groups of youth workers who meet monthly for lunch and to resource each other. This group really cares about students and taking care of youth workers.

If you don't live in an area with a good youth ministry network, my advice is to start one. All it takes is two people coming together to share resources, and you officially have a network. Here are some of the great benefits of networking.

Sharing Resources

So many churches and youth ministries possess stuff they just don't use all the time. If you network with others, you can ask to borrow their stuff. Need a portable sound system? I bet someone in your network has one and will let you borrow it. The network is a great place to come up with lists of stuff each person has, making sure that everyone knows who to ask when they need something.

Sharing Space

This is often an issue in youth ministry. You want to do something cool for your students, but you just don't have the right place to do it. What if you partnered with another church's youth ministry and used their facility for an event or retreat? Students usually enjoy going somewhere different for youth ministry activities, if only for the novelty or the change—and you can likely borrow a room or a space from someone in your network for free. Think about doing an all-nighter where you drive around to different youth ministry rooms where each church has a specific set-up highlighting what they're good at. Sort of like a progressive "dinner" at various spaces—except the food is youth ministry.

Partnering to Pull Off Events
You Can't Do Alone

Many of us wish we could do certain events, except we just don't have the resources to pull them off. Maybe we want to bring in speakers or bands or do all-nighters, but on our own we just can't make them happen. However, if you partner with other churches, your network may be able to pull them off. It's also way more fun if you can rent out the whole bowling alley or skating rink for a concert and watch the room get packed to capacity than it is when you have just a few bowling lanes filled or only part of a room occupied. The kids will feel that added energy when the space is full.

Sharing Transportation Costs

You've got to think of transportation as part of the event or trip. If you've got a retreat coming up, chances are you might be in the vehicles for a couple of hours to the retreat center and back. Partnering with other churches in your network might be a great way to shrink the costs. Maybe another church has vehicles you don't. Partnering in that case might bring your costs down to almost nothing.

Recently I was going to a youth worker training event. I let my network in Dallas know that I was driving there, and if anyone wanted to come along they could climb in the van for free. We ended up taking seven youth workers from Dallas who alone wouldn't have been able to attend the event.

Speaking at Each Other's Events

Sometimes your students need a break from hearing you speak—sometimes *you* need a break from hearing you speak (or at least a break from the work involved in prepping a talk). Maybe within your network there are some great people who can step in and speak at an event. Bringing in outside speakers typically has costs associated with it, so this approach can be a way of doing it for cheap. And if you swap speaking at each other's camps, you could potentially save quite a bit of money. And what a great way to bless another youth ministry by helping them out in this way!

Partnering for Training Events

Going to big youth ministry training events can be expensive, and bringing in some of those top-notch speakers/trainers to your home turf can be as well. But when you split the costs for the network, it's much more feasible.

At a recent network lunch we brought in a nationally known youth ministry speaker/trainer. There were about 40 of us at the lunch, and it was a great learning time. Many of the churches represented had part-time or volunteer youth workers who'd never think about bringing in a trainer. But as a network we had a few people with the resources to make it happen, and it benefited all of the Dallas youth workers involved. Because we had so many people at the event, a vendor offered to provide lunch for us.

Benefiting from Others' Strengths

I tell people in my network all the time that I want to use my experience, skills, gifts, and resources to help. I'm very serious about this, and people take me up on my offer pretty frequently. Biblically speaking, we exist to help each other. In my network there are people who've been doing youth ministry way longer than me. I've had great conversations with them about my dreams and ideas, and they've shown me how to pull off things in the Dallas area that I'd never have thought of simply because they've gone through things here before me.

We must recognize that youth workers collectively possess varied strengths; often they just want to be used. It doesn't take much more than a cup of coffee, a phone call, or a lunch together in order to figure out how each of your youth ministries can benefit from the others—and vice versa.

Kicking Ideas Around

For me, this is a huge benefit of my network. It's easy to let blinders slip on and see only what's directly in front of you. This happens with planning and dreaming a lot. We get stuck in ruts, thinking about our churches, students, and ministries, forgetting to think bigger than our little bubbles. Which is why a network can be a valuable place to sit down with other youth workers and bounce ideas off each other. As a shoestring approach this is huge. For instance, if I tell others I'm thinking about doing something, my fellow network folks might have great ideas about how to do it cheaper or with fewer resources than I'd originally planned.

Identifying with Like-Minded People

Similar to the previous benefit, I find that simply relating to others who do what I do and think about how to love teenagers like I do is a huge resource in and of itself. I don't have to explain myself all the time (e.g., "You're a . . . *youth worker*?" "When do you get to be a *real* pastor?"). They get me already. I also don't have to explain all of my ideas or plans—they understand. The shoestring principle here is that I'm not wasting time trying to get other people on board with what I'm thinking. My network generally gets it pretty quickly and thinks the way I do, therefore it's easy to get to the root of the need and figure out solutions.

Your Challenge

Start making a list of people with whom you already network or with whom you *want* to network. How can you benefit each other? What resources do you have that you could share with other youth ministries?

Network

chapter 9

The Congregation

The Shoestring Benefits

Chap Clark often shows a picture of youth ministry in most churches as a one-eared Mickey Mouse. The idea is that youth ministry is typically just *slightly* connected to the rest of the church. There are huge shoestring benefits to overcoming this tendency because the rest of your church might be an incredible underutilized resource. In many congregations people would love to step in and help the youth department, but they don't simply because they don't know what you need, don't feel as though they have anything to offer, or are often just scared of you and your kids. The following are some ways to end this trend.

Volunteers/Sponsors

Let's get this out of the way first. Yes, you should be helping to get the church involved in students' lives. You should be asking people to volunteer in the youth ministry—and not just poor college students. Some of our older congregants are actually better suited to volunteer and love teens because their real jobs and stable lives often mean they can do more, not less. But you must give them specific tasks and goals so they sense more tangibly that they're actually being used. You'll benefit from a mix of older and younger volunteers because they can help take care of each other, too.

Sunday School Classes

I mentioned this previously, but it bears repeating—and augmenting. Most Sunday school classes have goals related to "outreach" projects a few times a year. What if the youth ministry went to them and asked if they would sponsor an event? You could ask them to help with a youth fundraiser or redesigning the youth room. What if they said they wanted to help cover the costs of sending students on a summer missions project or help pay for transportation for summer camp? The key is asking them to help with a *specific* task that they can easily get behind and support.

Lists of Needs

One action I've found over the years that's proven helpful and effective is circulating through your congregation a list of things that the youth department needs. Sort of like a Christmas list, I just catalog everything we happen to need. You'd be surprised by how many people are willing to donate and provide resources that are on your list. Rarely is the issue a general unwillingness to help out; more often it's that others in the church don't know what the youth ministry needs, so they don't know how to help. If you go this route, you also might want to set up a good database that can connect resource needs with people who have those resources, so that when you need something, all you have to do is look at your list and make some phone calls.

Your Challenge

What groups at your church do you need to reach out to? What would you have them do? Start working on a "list of needs" right now and get that to your congregation.

The Congregation

chapter 10

Friends and Family

The Shoestring Benefits

As with people in your church, in most cases friends and family members are willing to step in and help but just don't know what you need. Chances are you have friends who support what you do in youth ministry; well, it's time to start utilizing some of your friends to help out when you have a need. In a similar way most parents and other family members of your students have the same goal as you. They all love their kids and want to help out however they can. In many youth ministries we underutilize the resources of friends, parents, and families. So the following is a list of some ways you might want to use them.

Parents as Volunteers

We have parents come with us on many of our retreats, mission projects, camps, and events. In general most of our parents just sign up and pay and come with us. We don't pay for them to come because many have the resources to cover their own costs. This is a huge benefit because it gets us more adults on trips to help, but we're not using the budget or passing on the costs to students. It makes the trips safer, cheaper, and the intergenerational piece is a very big added benefit.

Parents as Speakers and Program Leaders

Instead of paying for speakers to attend our recent ski trip, we had our staff and some parents put together the program. There is a huge benefit because students often see these adults around the church, and after they hear them talk about their faith journeys or some other aspect of Christianity, that helps forge a connection between them and your teens—a win for your ministry. I'm betting you've got some great parents in your church who have amazing stories to tell or talents to lead. Why not give them a shot? It certainly fits the shoestring approach, and it's a great model for getting parents involved.

Parents as "Snack Masters"

Parents want to provide for students, and sometimes giving them the simple task of organizing snacks goes a long way to filling a big need cheaply. We do two trips a year for which we ask parents to provide snacks. The response is generally overwhelming, and usually we get more stuff than we know what to do with (which carries the added benefit of saving nonperishable snacks we don't need for an immediate event so we have it for future gigs). Snacks are expensive but spreading the cost among a bunch of families really drops the price for them— and can bring the cost down to zero for your ministry.

Parents and Friends as "Resource Kings and Queens"

In most cases parents have been around a lot longer than you have. That means their networks and resources are probably much bigger than yours. So get their help. They might have connections that you don't that would help lower costs. They might know the right people who're willing to help them help you, only because of their relationships with these key folks—relationships that you don't have. In my youth ministry are parents who sit on the boards of a lot of local organizations, so I take note of those connections—and when I need something, I often go to them.

Your Own Friends

Don't forget that your friends like you. That's why they are your friends. They also know what you do. Therefore it's totally okay to ask them to help you occasionally. They may not be your top volunteers, but they may be willing to help run a retreat or an activity once in a while. Again you just have to ask them.

Your Challenge

What types of activities or events have you asked your parents/friends to be part of or help with? What resources do they possess that you don't? What are some new areas with which you could ask them to help?

_____

_____

_____

_____

_____

_____

_____

_____

_____

_____

_____

_____

_____

_____

_____

_____

_____

_____

_____

chapter 11

Parachurch Ministries

The Shoestring Benefits

Working with local parachurch ministries can provide the same kinds of results and benefits as working with a youth ministry network. But parachurch partnerships carry potential additional benefits worth looking at, too. They generally have some pretty great networks of their own and often resources that are bigger than what's available to you through your local youth ministry network. A good example of this is Young Life and their extensive network of camps all over the United States. Through such networks you may encounter additional resources for your arsenal that you wouldn't otherwise have access to. The following are a few additional thoughts.

Specific Focus

Often a parachurch ministry is all about a specific ministry focus—one that can be helpful to your church. Consider parachurch ministries such as Athletes in Action or Fellowship of Christian Athletes; they each have a long track record of great success reaching student athletes. So instead of you bringing in speakers to reach those kids for your own ministry or trying to pull off a baseball game night when most of your group isn't interested, you can save a lot of money by partnering with such a parachurch ministry, giving your own athletes the opportunity to benefit from their resources. In a similar way, Young Life is often better at reaching non-Christian students on campus than most youth ministries; perhaps partnering with them could save you a lot of financial resources you might have been planning to use on a camp.

Partnerships

The last several years we've been unable to fill a bus for our annual ski retreat. So we finally partnered with a parachurch ministry that a number of our staff used to work for, and as a result we provided a great ski retreat for both groups. In our case one of the leaders of the parachurch ministry had been running ski retreats for a long time and knew the ins and outs of how to successfully create budgets for them. The parachurch ministry also had connections to speakers who would come and volunteer their time. All of these partnering factors saved us money and allowed us to pull off a trip we otherwise couldn't do alone.

Shared Space

For many years we've opened up our youth room for parachurch ministries to use; we often do this for free and bless them with our resource. This has been a huge win for us. One night Young Life borrowed our youth room and brought in a big-name musical act—along with six busloads of students. Our kids were invited as well, which was huge in many ways—including the fact that the whole event was essentially free for us. The room was packed, and our students felt as though we did something amazing.

Your Challenge

What parachurch ministries are in your town? Have you built relationships with any of them? How can you partner with them?

chapter 12

Camps, Colleges, Seminaries

The Shoestring Benefits

This is an area I believe we in the youth ministry world underutilize the most! There are so many resources connected to these three entities that can benefit your youth ministry. And believe it or not, most camps, colleges, and seminaries *want* to partner with you and your youth ministry and your church. Maybe you can become a place where they try out their summer program ideas. Maybe they need to place some interns in a great youth ministry program. The possibilities are numerous.

Camps

Facilities

Most camps aren't full all year long. Sure they're packed during the summer months and winter weekends, but in between those times they generally have plenty of open spaces. Did you know that most Christian camps will give you a cabin during the week for whatever you need if you just call them up and ask for it? It's true! Camps need people to come in as campers. They need people to staff the camp, too. They see you as a resource, and they want to take care of you.

You should also be aware that camps enjoy visitors. So grab your team and visit a local camp for the day. Get them to give you a tour and see what resources they have to offer. They may even feed you and give you space to conduct a planning retreat while you're there. Again they need you and want to resource you.

A cheap way of doing a retreat is to take your kids to camp to work for a weekend. Most camps operate some sort of "wait" staff in their dining halls and, in exchange for a few hours a day of serving and cleaning, you might get a fully paid weekend retreat. That's shoestring-y for sure! Another thing to think about, again, is to partner with another youth ministry to rent out a camp; such a route can significantly lower your costs.

Staff

Camp staff members are great people, and they get really bored just sitting in their offices planning things. If you have an established relationship with a camp, you might want to ask if some of their people can come to your youth group every now and then as a resource.

What about having camp staffers teach a weekend in the fall to reinforce ideas students heard at summer camp a few months earlier? What if they came to run a special game students learned at camp? Most camp staff members are pretty good at running "camp," too. So if you're doing something on your own, you could call them up and take them to lunch and probably glean some really great ideas from them. Remember, again, most camps exist to partner with the church, so a big part of their job is to do just that. They often recruit staff from churches—so help them out and open up your church for a recruiting stop so they can come in and speak or lead games.

Stuff

One thing I loved about working at camp is the sheer number of toys we had to play with. Most camps have a ton of stuff sitting in closets that don't get used very much. If you have the resources to pick things up, some camps may let you borrow their stuff for free for a weekend retreat. We once borrowed those giant globes in which you can put kids and roll them around a field. I have no idea what it costs to own them, but all I did was call and ask if I could borrow them—and it worked.

Colleges

Facilities

Similar to camps, colleges generally have some pretty great facilities that during certain times of year are not used very much. This summer my youth group is embarking on a mission trip to a U.S. city and staying at a Christian college campus. We're also eating all of our meals at the college. As noted previously, this approach is much cheaper than staying in a hotel and much more comfortable than sleeping on a church floor. Most colleges have great facilities that you can rent. We've rented gyms, pools, meeting rooms, and used many of their outdoor spaces.

It's an added plus if your church has a relationship with a college because you can give them access to the church for college recruiting in exchange for using some of their space. Some colleges have pretty great outdoor programs and might be willing to work with you to give you access to equipment or other things as well.

Staff/Faculty

Again, some amazing people work at colleges. If it's a Christian college, you might build a relationship with whoever teaches or chairs the youth ministry program or is in charge of internships. I've benefited greatly from relationships with colleges over the years and have provided internships at my youth group for college students as well as been blessed by some high-quality (and free) help.

Beyond Christian colleges you might find staff or faculty members who could prove to be great academic resources—perhaps they could guest lecture about specific topics. You might also meet some great people who are particularly passionate about getting students outdoors or love serving in the city. You never know what type of great shoestring-y resources you'll find among people on college campuses.

Stuff

Again don't be afraid to ask. A college I was involved with had an amazing outdoor program, and we always asked to borrow their equipment. Once they realized they could trust me, they let us borrow whatever we wanted, and as we continued building relationships many of the outdoor staff would come with us (for free) when we planned trips because they knew we were a lot of fun. I've borrowed vehicles, sound equipment, sports equipment, outdoor equipment. You just have to find the right person and ask.

Seminaries

Facilities

I've always done ministry in close proximity to seminaries. In many cases seminaries are more than willing to let local churches use their facilities. We've used meeting spaces, libraries, outdoor areas, prayer gardens, dining halls, and classrooms—all for free. Remember that seminaries generally exist to do the same thing as your local church, so see what kind of mutually beneficial relationship you can put together. At one church I worked at, the seminary used our sanctuary for graduation every year—and because of that relationship we generally could do whatever we wanted on their campus.

Faculty/Staff/Students

I don't know of any seminary from which you can graduate without getting some sort of practical ministry experience. Students need internships or other hands-on opportunities to put what they're learning into practice. Every year we have a local seminary bring in their entire class to observe our youth ministry for a night. Afterward we do a big roundtable discussion and answer questions. In addition we have an extensive internship program in which seminary students work 20 hours a week and get paid a little just to be involved in students' lives. I've also partnered with local seminaries and other churches to bring in guest speakers and host parenting classes and training events. There are so many great faculty and staff who love the church, too, that this is a great way of getting help really inexpensively—or for free.

Stuff

Seminaries get a bad rap in the "practical" department. Most of us probably haven't spent a lot of time thinking about what theological institutions have that we can use. But don't underestimate seminaries. Fuller Seminary had some great resources, including a solid relationship with several retreat centers and monasteries; I used those connections for some youth retreats. I also lived in a great old house the seminary owned (as did a certain theologian of some renown, Dr. Tony Jones), and we often used that space to host youth ministry events and Bible studies—a kind of theological frat house. So don't underestimate seminaries' resources (but again, you have to ask them for their help).

Your Challenge

What camps, colleges, and seminaries are around that you could partner with? Who do you know at these places? What needs do you have that they might be able to help with? How do you suppose you might benefit them, too?

chapter 13

Training Organizations

The Shoestring Benefits

Many groups out there are resourcing the youth ministry world. Some conferences cost quite a bit of money but still may be totally worth it. There are also ways of training for cheap—and sometimes even for free. I assume that you want to do training; so instead of telling you which ones to consider, I'll simply offer some general principles on how to make training cheaper.

Partner at Conferences to Reduce Costs

Generally the more people you take to a conference, the better price you get. Therefore, always partner and bring that number. You'll also save money by splitting costs for transportation, food, and hotel rooms. It's not as relaxing to fill your hotel room with additional bodies, but if the goal is training on a shoestring, that's a way to do it.

Bringing in Resources Is Cheaper Than Going to Them

We've brought in a few nationally recognized speakers to my church to give talks on youth ministry topics. Sometimes it's possible to get someone at the church to pay for the whole thing. If you can get the right person to understand how it will benefit the whole church, you might get some funding from the church budget. We've also partnered with other local churches to split the costs—lots of benefit for much less money than attending a conference, especially if you focus on one or two topics that a single speaker could teach.

Resource the Whole Church, Not Just the Youth Ministry

We had a guest speaker a few years back who preached on a youth ministry topic during our 11 a.m. service; he'd teach on the same topic later that evening with our youth ministry families. But because he preached to the entire congregation, it paid off immensely for the youth ministry, as it opened the congregation's eyes a bit to what our youth ministry was all about—that we had a great plan for reaching students. As a result we received a lot of support from the rest of the church in the form of new volunteers and financial resources.

Some Organizations Have Valuable Niches

The Center for Youth Ministry Training (http.cymt.org) in Nashville partners with a few different seminaries. Their model is to bring in staff for three years and place them in churches in the Tennessee area, training, coaching, and teaching them. At the end of the three years, the staff members have fully paid-for master's degrees in youth ministry. That's a great resource if you have some post-college students who want to do youth ministry and get a seminary degree but don't know how to go about it.

Organizations such as Barefoot offer what they call $5 Youth Ministry training (see $5 training at www.barefoottraining.com) where they bring in a speaker to a specific area to training events. Youth Specialties holds regional events such as YSPalooza (www.yspalooza.com) and the National Youth Workers Convention (www.nywc.com) where they bring in speakers and have a great focus on the "family" of youth ministry people. You'll need to figure out what organization you want to work with first and then start looking at how to do it for cheaper.

Consultants

The word *consultant* just sounds like it's going to cost a lot. But in the long run a consultant often will save you big bucks. You might be contemplating doing something that will potentially cost a significant amount of money, but a consultant might give you different ideas and resources you can use to do the same thing for less money. There are some great consultants out there such as The Riddle Group (www.theriddlegroup.com) and Youth Ministry Architects (www.ymarchitects.com) that can help you do things in ways that will save you additional expenses.

Become the Expert
It may sound silly to say this, but often in the youth ministry world the greatest expert on a particular subject dealing with youth ministry is . . . *you.* You might want to take some time to develop your knowledge through training resources and seminars and in turn teach them to your volunteers, paid staff, parents, and church yourself. Although it takes more work, it is a shoestring-y way to provide training.

Local Friends and Resources
We've brought in a number of therapists, counselors, and seminary staff to train us over the years. In most cases they come in and train for free because it's great exposure for their ministries or practices.

Your Challenge
What organizations meet the needs of your youth, your youth ministry, your church, and your community? Think about what resources you can get someone else to pay for. Maybe a benefactor at your church is willing to cover training costs if you can demonstrate its value.

People/Partnerships That Can Bolster Your Shoestring Budget

chapter 14

Denominational Help

The Shoestring Benefits

In most cases if you're a part of a denomination or network of churches, then there's likely someone out there whose job it is to help resource your church. This isn't always the case, but in general it is. These people are often just waiting for you to call and ask for help.

My denomination has some full-time staff members who only do youth ministry. I've built some good relationships with them and feel very comfortable asking for help. Last year I went to a conference for free because I called my denomination and asked if it had any scholarship money available. In the same way your denomination may have grant or scholarship money available, or it can put you in touch with people who may help fund things. Your denomination also may be able to provide speakers who'll lead training events for you, or it may know of other local people within the denominational network who might be a good fit to help you out.

Also there may be a church in your denomination with a resource it isn't using anymore; perhaps it would be willing to ship it to you. Another way we've used our denomination is to simply ask to use its facilities when we're traveling anywhere with our group and need a cheap or free place to stay for the night.

Your Challenge

If you're part of a denomination, do you know the people whose job it is to help you? Have you spoken to any of them on the phone and told them your needs? Is there any sort of email list or Web site you can join that might provide you with resources that can benefit your youth ministry?

chapter 15

Other Ministries in Your Church

The Shoestring Benefits

In an earlier chapter I talked about the benefits of getting the "congregation" involved in the youth ministry. In this chapter I want to highlight other ministry areas of the church that could provide for the youth ministry; their strengths might be the cheapest alternative.

Counseling

Our church has an in-house counseling service and a referral program. Often in the youth ministry world we don't know how to handle certain issues that come up or to whom to refer people. If your church has a counseling ministry, that might be the first step toward providing free or inexpensive resources to people who need it. We have a team of three therapists who teach a monthly Sunday morning parenting class. They cover a lot of topics, and it doesn't cost our youth ministry a thing. Our therapists do it as a way to serve the church, and they benefit from receiving referrals.

Finance

One area youth ministers are notoriously bad at is managing finances. Going over budget or incurring unexpected expenses can severely jeopardize a mission trip. Fortunately many churches have finance departments willing to help and love it when they're asked how to put together budgets. You might also find that when they know you care about doing things the right way financially, they're willing to help you out with funds you didn't even know you had. Financial planning is a great shoestring model.

Financial Teaching

We use a ministry at our church called Crown Financial Planning to teach our students about money. We had about 12 volunteers from this ministry teach a four-week series to our seventh through 12th graders, complete with small groups. It was done in a way that we never could have duplicated with just the youth staff, and it was free.

Missions

If you do youth group mission trips, partnering with your church missions department is a huge win. Chances are good the department has people who've been doing missions for a long time and can probably help you save money. They may have tips and tricks they can share that will help you raise financial support, find cheap transportation, and even know donors who'd be willing to help fund part of your trip. They also can step in and train your teams and might have books and resources you can use (instead of you having to buy them).

Sports/Outdoors

Many churches have a sports and outdoor ministries. If you aren't (also) the person in charge of that area, you should make friends with that individual and utilize this ministry to help you augment camps, retreats, and events. Your church's sports/outdoor ministry might have some great equipment and resources that could benefit your ministry—and again you don't have to buy stuff.

Adults

I've covered this previously, but it's so important to repeat: *There are adults at your church who want to help . . . but don't know what to do and have never been asked!* What about partnering with your adult or senior adult ministries to do something that on your own you couldn't do? These adult ministries likely have resources unavailable to you—and they also probably know how to pull things off you couldn't on your own. I've found that often these adults have dreams and ideas that they want to make realities—and the youth ministry may just help them make those dreams happen. So invite them to help and give them real tasks.

Communications

Chances are that your church has a communications person or department. And okay, maybe the folks there don't create the hippest logos or the best designs, but maybe they know someone who can create more of what you're after. One thing for sure is these people are charged with communicating things at your church, and in general they're probably the experts. So you should try to use them. Even if you design your own flyers, they may have resources to print them more inexpensively.

My church's bulletin always comes with one extra blank page—and if my flyer is added to that blank page, it costs me less than 20 percent of what it would have cost if I printed the page myself. I'm great at communicating to youth and families, but the communications department is great at communicating to the *whole church*. They also employ avenues of communication that I don't have access to, or they can think about how to help us in ways that I don't. For example, in regard to the TV monitors that scroll ads around our church, I can't put anything on them—but they can . . . and it's free!

Your Challenge

Set up meetings with other ministries in your church and see how you could collaborate with them to do "more for less." What areas of the church might have great resources for the youth department?

_____

_____

_____

_____

_____

_____

People/Partnerships That Can Bolster Your Shoestring Budget

PART 3

Intangibles
That Can Bolster Your

EARLIER IN THE BOOK I noted that the youth ministry-on-a-shoestring approach is more of a lifestyle than a program. It's almost a methodology for looking at something, not with your normal glasses but with your shoestring glasses, and asking the question "How can I do more for less?"

That idea follows in this new section. When I first worked on these chapters, I kept trying to find a better word to use than *intangibles*, but the more I tried to find just the right word, the more convinced I was that there's no better way to explain these principles.

The principles that we will talk about in the next several chapters are not basic youth ministry. Some are principles you figure out as you fail; others will take some major rethinking on your part to figure out and apply to your own context.

One thing, though, is for certain: In your ministry context all of these principles and more can be resources that will help you pull off things in ways you never thought possible—in ways you never expected. If you take advantage of these intangibles, chances are good that you can do things for less money, too. Not everything will apply to your context but hopefully something will resonate with you and help your ministry.

Keep in mind that there are negative and positive sides to all of these resources, and you'll have to figure out how best to balance them with your resources of stuff and people/partnerships.

As with previous chapters, when you get to the end of each chapter in this section, there will be a bit of space for you to note some of the intangible resources available to you that could help you do more for less in your youth ministry context.

chapter 16

History

How can "history" save you money and help you to do more for less? In a world that values quick change and looks for the next big thing, it can be hard to understand how history can be a valuable shoestring resource.

Here's a quick example: My youth ministry does one annual fundraiser. It's a pancake breakfast for the entire congregation. It doesn't take a lot of resources or work to pull off, and it gets great results. Everyone at the church knows what it's for. Everyone knows it happens in November. Parents and families know what we need them to do, and we raise a lot of money for a very specific purpose—youth missions.

The "history" of that event is a huge resource for us. Why? Because we don't have to promote it or try to explain it—everybody's familiar with its history. Everyone's already on board and knows what they need to do. If we tried to do a different fundraiser or add a new event, we may not raise the money we need. Why? Because there's no history surrounding the new fundraiser. The same can be said for a specific camp we do every year. There's great history behind the camp, and everyone knows the resources we need to pull it off. Families step up to help, and because of that we can do things more inexpensively. Maybe you're new at your church, or you don't have this type of history. Well, you can still start right now building these types of events and expectations. The following are some additional ideas.

Church Leaders Who Used to Do Youth Ministry

A few times a year my senior pastor says from the pulpit that he loves and believes in youth ministry. He has a long history of being involved in youth ministry, and his statements from the pulpit go a long way toward helping our youth ministry acquire the resources we need in order to do things for less. For example, when he says he loves youth ministry and believes we should support it, our missions fundraiser generally goes much better.

Your senior leaders who have a history with youth ministry also have relationships with critical people in the church who you don't know—so if you need what these people have, youth ministry-friendly senior leaders in your corner can help you find the people resources you need. Use their history and knowledge of youth ministry to benefit your ministry now.

Former Students Who Could Return as Volunteers

Hopefully you've been blessed with students who've graduated from the youth group but want to return to serve as volunteer leaders. In the last several years we've been pushing a volunteer model in our youth department. These former students—especially if they've participated in specific mission trips or have been involved in the nuts and bolts of your ministry—can be a huge resource for you.

Often their main reason for wanting to return is that specific trips or aspects of the youth ministry changed their lives, and they want youth to experience the same life-change (plus, they're great at promoting and publicizing trips). The history they can relate to younger students helps us get more of them involved, which can often make a trip or event cheaper as the cost is spread out.

In addition, a lot of our high schoolers are actively involved in leading our younger grades. This pays off immensely for us, too, as the parents of most of these student leaders pay their way for trips and other activities so we don't need to dip into our budget. There's an added benefit for student leaders as well, since they receive credit for service hours that they can refer to on college applications.

Parents with Long-Term Roles

Parents whose children have gone through or are in the youth ministry are great history resources. They're the ones who've probably been at the church and in the youth ministry longer than you and can use that history to help you do things for less. Maybe they remember a great camp facility rented years ago that's also pretty cheap. Maybe they've had specific roles on ski trips for years and fully expect to be used in those ways. They might have more connections in the community to resources than you do as well.

Our high schoolers have been doing Jamaica mission trips running for years. Parents fully understand the importance of it and know how it's helped shape their children's lives. When we promote those trips, many of those parents' stories and history with Jamaica are our best resources for getting needed support. A parent committee can often be the best resource in this area because when you provide a place for them to dialogue and kick around ideas, they'll often come up with resources you never thought of.

A Congregation That Understands the Vision

As I shared in the intro to this section, we have some great history with a fundraising event that our whole congregation gets behind. The history of that event and a congregation that fully understands where that money goes is a huge win for us. More than that, though, we try to make sure that our whole congregation understands what we're trying to do within the youth department. For me it's a huge win to overhear someone in the congregation explain to someone else the goals and vision of our youth ministry. If your congregation is sold on what you're doing, then you'll have great support from them (and they'll let you use your resources, which again, will make things cheaper).

A Great Experience Replicates Itself

While we do change things up regularly, we have a few specific events that we do every year—and the history of these annual events gives us great momentum for when we do want to try something different. For example we do an annual "don't miss" junior high event called Polar Bear. It's gone on for more than 10 years, and because of the history of it, we can count on a few specific things to save money. The first is that we ask parents to provide all the snack food for the weekend—but after so many years of success, parents stop by our youth facility in the two weeks before the event and drop off tons of snacks. Secondly, this is one of those events where older students want to come back and lead because they know how great it is—so our high school seniors actually pay to come back and be leaders.

Use Community and City Events

When I was a youth pastor in Los Angeles, every year Fuller Theological Seminary asked us to help them save 300 seats on the Rose Bowl parade route for their big donors. What that required was for us to have 300 students spend the night on the parade route taking up space on the sidewalk, and then at 6 a.m. we would set up 300 chairs. Fuller paid us quite a bit of money to do that every year, and it always went to missions.

In the same way, your community or city may sponsor events you can piggyback on. For instance, we let the local high school use our youth room twice a year for two events. They promote, sponsor, decorate, and pay for both events, but we tell our students and staff they should be a part of the events as well. In the end we have the opportunity to be with hundreds of students at events that took us no money or time to set up. That's a huge win for us and very much a shoestring-model strategy.

Shoestring Challenge

What are some "historical" resources at your church that could save you money? How might you utilize some of these in your next round of event planning? If you don't have many resources in this category, how can you go about building some?

_____

_____

_____

_____

_____

_____

_____

History

chapter 17

Longevity/ Relational Equity

FEELING AS THOUGH you have no available resources is a tough place to be and can lead to a lot of frustration and discontent. Leaders with big ideas and plans but little understanding of resources will always feel like they're butting against a ceiling of what they can do. This is one of the primary reasons, in my opinion, that youth workers leave ministry after a few years. Leaders who last in youth ministry recognize all the available resources around them and know how to utilize them.

Young youth workers are often taught, too, that the only resource the church, families, and students care about is *them*. This can lead to youth ministers working unhealthy hours trying to be all things to all people. Take, for example, the 24-year-old youth worker who leads four small groups, sets up the sound system, writes the curriculum, cleans up after meetings, plans camps, goes to lunches at the public schools, maintains the ministry Web site and anything else available to take on because in his mind, he's the only resource available to the youth ministry. But if the church pushes this view, it will most likely cycle through youth workers every couple of years. This model isn't sustainable for leaders who want to live healthy lives.

Some of the best youth ministry leaders who've been around for the longest stretches know that they can't be the only resources for their youth ministries. They know about all the "stuff" around them they can use to do ministry and know that to last in the youth ministry world they have to use this stuff. They don't feel pressure to do it all themselves and commonly have pretty big tool kits—address books full of people to call on, brains full of ideas, closets full of resources . . . and they can always find the perfect thing for the job right at the perfect time.

Shoestring Challenge

What relationships at your church are helpful in your youth ministry? Have you fully given leadership opportunities to those engaged in your ministry? What resources does your longevity (or the longevity of your ministry) offer you that you need to use?

chapter 18

Failures/ Successes

FAILURES AND SUCCESSES can both be used as resources if you manage them correctly. In the case of successes, any great event, camp, mission trip, or activity can itself be the "advertisement" that encourages more people to support it the following year. The buzz generated by participants can engage others to provide resources. Failures can also be big helps, as long as you evaluate what went wrong and what resources would have helped make them successes.

Successes

It's a good idea after an event to make sure your families, staff, congregation, and senior leadership have a good picture of what went well. This is especially important if someone provided resources for the event.

This year we had a family provide a significant donation to reduce the cost of our annual high school ski trip. I kept the family in the loop during the whole planning process, and then after the trip I let them know the impact their donation had.

I also want to make sure I effectively communicate to the whole church about how we're reaching our goals and changing students' lives. A big part of our job, post-event, is publicizing the great things that happened at the event. Again, this will encourage more people to get on board and be part of helping with the same event the following year.

Failures as Positives

Some failures can be positives—especially if they're the result of a lack of resources. For instance, if you can say something like, "We had only a few kids go this year because it was so expensive, but we're fully committed to this model because if we just had more resources, we could do it, and it would be phenomenal."

I said that after our ski trip last year. Last year the trip cost twice as much money. Many of our kids couldn't attend. We were convinced if we could get the trip cost down to a certain price-point per attendee, then we'd be able to fill a bus and get more kids involved. Because I was convinced how important this ski trip is and felt as though our goals were solid, I simply began asking people to help us pull it off. Then someone stepped up financially, we were able to do the trip for the lower price, and it was a huge success.

Failures as Negatives

Some failures will teach you to never do that event again. Maybe you missed it and really didn't have a good vision or idea for that camp. The shoestring principle here is to learn from that failure and avoid repeating it—especially in cases when you lost money.

Don't try to do something just because everyone else does it. If you experience a failure, it might be because you simply shouldn't have done it. So . . . don't do it again (and save money!). Figure out something else. Because the worst kind of failure is when you try the same thing again and get the same bad results.

Shoestring Challenge

What successes have you experienced in your youth ministry that you can build on? Are there specific events that have gone so well that you now have a great platform for asking for more resources? What failures have you experienced? Did you communicate the vision and ideas well enough? How might you be able to use that failure to find more resources—or at least learn from it?

Failures/Successes

chapter 19

Dreams and Aspirations

THIS IS ONE OF THOSE INTANGIBLE ELEMENTS that might take a minute to get but is something that will go a long way toward helping you do youth ministry on a shoestring budget.

Years ago my senior pastor challenged me to try to out-dream him. At the time I was pretty entrenched in doing ministry in a particular way, so it seemed like a waste of time to start dreaming. But the more I watched him have success, the more I got it. My pastor's premise was that you have to start with dreams and then try to figure out how to make them happen. The shoestring approach to this says that you want to do trips, events, missions, and camps—so you need to start dreaming, putting into practice tangible approaches to making them a reality. This is the opposite of what I call the "Eeyore problem"—in other words, when people are so focused on their problems and limitations that they can't spend any time dreaming.

I've worked over the years with a number of people with amazing dreams, and I always tell them that if they come to me with a dream, I'll help them figure out ways to make them realities. You might be amazed at the people around you who catch the same dream and step up to make it happen.

Make Your Dreams Big

There's no reason to limit your dreams because you have no resources. If anything, having no resources makes your dreams even bigger!

I grew up in a little church with almost no budget. My youth pastor had a simple dream—that we'd have a summer camp every year. Dreams are simply scenarios you make up in your head about what you'd love to do. But it's amazing to observe how two groups of people with the same resources have vastly different results because one group dreams big and one group dreams small! My youth pastor knew we had no money in the budget, but he always pulled off "summer camp." Mostly these were less-expensive hiking or biking trips, yet I have great memories. The shoestring approach in this case is to start with the dream and then figure out how you can do it or something very similar to it with the resources you can find.

Get Others Involved in Your Dreams

Much of the shoestring approach to ministry involves collaboration and partnerships. You sitting in your office coming up with dreams is a good first step, but getting others on board with those dreams—and even making them their own dreams—is the next great step. Maybe there are resources and ideas out there that you don't know about—but if you get others to join your "dream team," perhaps those resources suddenly become available to you.

Create Realistic Plans to Accomplish Dreams

You might not be the person in your ministry who is able to create realistic plans and lists of how to accomplish dreams. Maybe you are just the dreamer and if that's the case you need a "go-to" person who can step in and help turn those into reality. I'll be the first to admit that I am a bit of a dreamer and a visionary and I need hands-on people who can create concrete steps to making things happen. It might be parents, volunteers, other adults, or other congregants who can step in and either help make those dreams a reality or help shape those dreams so they are more realistic.

Encourage Others to Dream

When my senior pastor encouraged me to out-dream him years ago, I took that as a real challenge. Now I try to encourage people I work with to dream big as well. For instance, I typically approach "dream" discussions or meetings with questions such as, "Have you thought about . . ."

and this helps them continue to dream. Providing the freedom to others to dream goes a long way toward getting your team members to think in a shoestring way and not constantly limit themselves only to what resources they think are available.

Shoestring Challenge

If there was nothing stopping you, what three dreams for your youth ministry would completely fit your needs right now? Set up a "dream meeting" with others engaged in your youth ministry and try to dream as big as you can. Think about some of the resources you have available and try to dream in big ways regarding how you could use them.

chapter 20

Education

THIS MAY NOT SOUND like a very shoestring-y concept because education generally isn't cheap. But many of us have gone to school and are underutilizing the resources available to us from that time in our lives. And nowadays there are tons of free online education resources you should be checking out, as they may open up your brain to new-and-improved ways of doing youth ministry—and on the cheap. (I won't list all the available resources in this chapter because there's a good chance new and better resources will have come into existence between the time I'm writing these words and when you read them. The concepts are the keys.)

Professors and Other Students

Chances are that if you attended college or are now enrolled in a college, you've had or have some pretty smart people around you. In particular if you're taking (or took) any sort of youth ministry class, your professors or fellow students might be great resources. My advice is to ask questions, bounce ideas off them, and get help formulating things. (Hey, if you're already paying for the class, you might as well get the most help from it.)

In one seminary class I had to put together a comprehensive youth ministry plan. Since I was a church youth pastor, I based the model on my church. But putting in all those hours evaluating the ministry really opened the door for us to try new things in new ways, and we ended up reallocating resources—which saved us a lot of money.

School Library and Other Resources

If you have a shoestring budget you probably can't afford to buy a lot of resources. But you're in luck because most Christian colleges and seminaries with youth ministry programs probably have a pretty good selection of material. If you're a student, it's simple to check out books you need, read them, and return them. If you're not a student, often you can still check out books, but it's a little bit harder.

If you can't check out books, try to build relationships with students and then see if you can borrow their books. Also check if the youth ministry program has any free online resources; you might find lectures, articles, and even syllabi that can prove helpful in giving you shoestring ideas. If you've taken classes already, you might have some books on your shelf that you should reread now that you're no longer a student. You might learn more, enjoy the subject material more, and process the information better than you did when you were in school.

Alumni Organizations

I attended a small college that publishes a quarterly alumni magazine. Over the years I've always submitted a note to the magazine when I move or switch jobs. During that time I've found that my fellow alumni are a great resource. I never would have guessed that some of them would end up the way they did (and I'm sure they never would've guessed I'd become a career youth pastor). Finding resources can be as simple as contacting the alumni office, expressing a need, and allowing them to message people to see if they can help.

Audit a Youth Ministry, Education, or Recreation Course

Some of us ended up in youth ministry with very little or no training, and we're constantly just holding on. But if you live near a school that offers youth ministry, education, or recreation courses, you might want to consider auditing some. Generally you can do it relatively cheaply, and you could get some great help for your ministry setting.

Don't underestimate the value of non-youth ministry courses, either. Some of the most helpful courses I took in college were communications, education methods, and even sports and fitness. I learned quite a few skills through these classes that easily translate to my ministry today.

Use Your Education

This may sound silly, but you paid a lot of money for your education—
you should try to use what you learned. I often fall into the rut of wanting to bring in experts to teach students and parents—but the truth is
that I went to school so I could actually become one of those experts!
It can add some extra work to your plate, but you probably have some
great resources at your fingertips and in your head that you need to use.
So instead of just outsourcing training, why not take the time to think
about what you learned in school and what you actually can present to
your group or your families as a result of your education?

Blogs as Education and Collaboration

I read about 20 blogs a day. I formulate some of my best ideas and
thoughts through others' words. In general you can comment and
interact with the blogger pretty easily. I've gotten involved in some
collaborative online blogging projects, which I've found are great ways
to think about resources in new ways and often help me think about
doing things more inexpensively. There are some great youth ministry
blogs out there, too, whose posts I regularly send around to my volunteer teams.

Podcasts and Webinars

This is still a growing area, but you should scour the Web to see what
resources are out there for training and youth ministry ideas. Most
big youth ministry conferences record speakers with audio and often
video—so if you can't afford the big bucks to attend a conference, consider downloading the few talks you want to hear from the conference
Web page. This route is way cheaper than paying for food, hotel, travel,
and conference expenses.

Shoestring Challenge

What educational resources do you take advantage of? What are some
things you want or need to learn in the next year? How can you learn
that material in more inexpensive ways? What resources are available at
your school (current or former) that could help you do youth ministry
on a shoestring?

Intangibles That Can Bolster Your Shoestring Budget

_____

_____

_____

_____

_____

_____

_____

_____

_____

_____

_____

_____

_____

chapter 21

Pastoral/Church Leadership Support

ATTENTION YOUNG AND NEW YOUTH PASTORS: *This might be the most important tip in this book!* It's a shoestring tip in the sense that your senior leadership probably has resources that you don't—but it's also just a regular tip to always strive for. Don't ever view your job as simply loving kids—because another huge part of your job is advocating for those kids to the rest of the church. You need to make sure the whole pastoral team and church leadership understand that what you're doing is crucial not just to teens' spiritual growth but also to the growth of the church, now and in the future.

Pastoral Team Support = Congregational Support

I note this in another chapter, but I want to reemphasize it here. You need the entire pastoral team to be just that—a team—when it comes to the youth ministry. It's very important that they support you and what you're doing because they represent the rest of the church—and can get the rest of the church behind you. And making sure that the senior leadership understands what you're doing and gets behind it are huge steps toward making that happen.

If you recall, in my present church our senior pastor loves to talk about the youth ministry and how we're doing. I've heard him say to the church on numerous occasions how proud he is of us and what we're doing—and I know these are more than merely nice words, because I do tell him what's going on in the youth ministry, and he supports us. Recently we were planning to start something new, so I made sure that my pastor had a full understanding of it, as well as the opportunity to ask questions—and then when we launched, he became our biggest supporter. And with his support came the congregation and all their resources.

Pastors and Church Leadership Will Help If You Ask

I try to get all the senior leaders involved in our youth ministry about once annually. We're a relatively big church, so it's not always possible, but in general all the church leaders are willing to help. In fact, since almost every church ministry impacts the others, it's very important for us to engage with each other—because other church leaders can be very gifted and help your youth (and you, in turn, can help the other leaders' ministries).

Recently we took our youth ministry leadership team out of town. But instead of paying for a guest speaker to come in to lead our Sunday morning program, our children's pastor—who's been involved in the lives of all of our students—stepped in and led the Sunday morning program along with our contemporary worship director and a volunteer. All we had to do was ask, and they were more than willing to help.

Make Your Needs/Vision Known

I learned this one the hard way. In the large church where I serve, I'm very aware that I can't be at every meeting. Recently there were several meetings I was unable to attend during which they discussed the youth department and some of our budget issues. I did a poor job of making sure people at that meeting had a good picture of what we needed and why, so our funding request was denied. Had I simply taken the time to make sure that other leaders in the church fully understood our proposal, things probably would have gone much better.

The Church's Vision Is Paramount

This last point is important in that the church needs to know that the youth ministry believes it's part of the overall plan and vision of the church—not doing its own thing. One of the key values of our church is being an "intergenerational blessing," so as a youth ministry we try to make sure that we're always thinking about how to expose our students to the rest of our older congregation. Even though it's often tempting to look for younger leaders to appeal to teens, we try to follow our church's vision instead of creating our own. This goes a long way toward harmony with the rest of the church when we try to plan things, because often resources that wouldn't be available if it were viewed as just a "youth" event become more available to us when it's a church event.

For example, our youth department is sponsoring a trip to Israel. But we're purposely calling it an "intergenerational" trip and have reached out to our senior adults and singles ministries. Because we're following the overall vision for our church, our communications ministry decided to help us promote it through channels that we don't normally have available to us. Also resources for this trip have really opened up, I believe, because we decided to pursue our church's vision instead of creating our own.

Shoestring Challenge

Pick a senior leader at your church, take her to coffee, and share with her what you're trying to do in your youth ministry. First, see how well she understands your department. Later you can ask how well the youth ministry is doing at coming alongside the church's goals and vision. What resources might be more available to the youth ministry if you were supporting the church's vision more? Who among the church leadership could you be partnering with whom you haven't yet considered?

Intangibles That Can Bolster Your Shoestring Budget

_____

_____

_____

_____

_____

_____

_____

_____

_____

_____

_____

_____

chapter 22

Community Support

EARLIER IN THE BOOK I encouraged you to find out what physical resources the community has that you might be able to use. Now I want to talk about other types of community resources available to you that might be intangible but have great shoestring potential.

Partnerships

We try to partner with our local schools as much as we can. We provide our youth room several times a year to the local high school, which in turn gives us a good relationship with the school administration, as well as better access to the campus. For instance, our youth staff gets passes to all school sporting events; this represents a pretty significant savings, and we receive it because we regularly partner with the school and share resources.

Counselors/Coaches

The last few years we've experienced a number of difficult deaths in our community. So we've partnered with school counselors to provide additional support for affected students as well as spaces where students can meet with each other and with teachers and coaches (off school grounds). The school has received this partnership well, and now when something happens or when I need a resource, I have people on campus I can reach out to for help.

School Board/PTA

Last year the heads of the Parent-Teacher Association at the local high school and junior high also were parents of students in our youth ministry. So when they hosted regular parent-training nights at the schools, they often asked me what subjects they thought should be covered. They sponsored and paid for the speakers, and we just told the other parents of our youth ministry students that they should go—a great training event that didn't cost us anything!

How Does the Surrounding Community View Your Youth Ministry?

Word of mouth is still a huge way that things happen in my community. Right now we have a pretty good reputation as a solid youth ministry with a great focus on missions and service. Parents talk about us to other parents, and in the end a number of students and families get involved because of our good reputation. That's shoestring-y because the more students who get involved, the lower the costs for everyone.

Shoestring Challenge

How often do you interact with the schools and actually partner with them? What is the nature of your relationship with local school leadership and/or the PTA? How might you need to reach out to the community more?

PART 4

Practical Planning
on a Shoestring
Budget

THIS SECTION IS TITLED "Practical Planning" because it offers a few models of how to think in a shoestring-y manner when you plan events. Remember: As I note throughout this book, the shoestring approach is a *mindset*. Therefore not all of these tips and ideas will necessarily work in your area. No one has every kind of resource at the ready, so in this section I unpack a few models we traditionally use in the youth ministry world and then encourage you to return to the first three sections and determine what resources you have covered under the "Stuff, People, and Intangibles" categories that help you do "more for less."

The best way to use this section is to not get the idea in your head that it will actually help plan your events for you. My goal is just to get you thinking about what resources are available to you and to help you creatively kick around ideas.

My shoestring advice: I encourage you to brainstorm a ton! Pull out a blank sheet of paper and start writing out all the resources available to you as you plan your event or activity. Don't disregard anything, because ideas can build upon each other.

chapter 23

Lock-Ins on a Shoestring

MOST YOUTH PASTORS have done lock-ins of some sort—fun, crazy nights that allow us to hang out with students for a large chunk of concentrated time. In planning lock-ins, often the first question we ask ourselves is, "How much can we charge?" Once we feel like we've figured out how much money we have to work with, then we can start planning activities.

I'm advocating that the shoestring youth ministry model doesn't start with the money question but instead begins asking a resource question: What resources are available that we could use?

Traditional Models

Most churches typically use two lock-in models:

Model 1
Students are carted off to a big, expensive "Fun Zone" where they spend the night with their friends playing mini-golf, laser tag, rock climbing, etc. Chances are good, too, that they'll have some bad pizza and all-you-can-drink sodas. To get them to this lock-in, the youth pastor will either charter a bus or vans.

Resource Problems of Model 1

1. Expensive
2. Leader dependent
3. Need to find/rent a "Fun Zone"
4. Focuses on activities, not relationships or group building
5. Safety issues in carting students around town

Model 2

Likely the more traditional lock-in involves students coming to church and typically not leaving the church for the majority of the night. Usually there are a lot of activities inside the church, but generally the focus is on what you can do with what's available. This is more of a shoestring lock-in model, but you can still do great lock-ins, even with a shoestring budget.

Resource Problems of Model 2

1. Dependent on facility
2. Can't always be rowdy in a church building (lots of church rules)
3. Not always the most exciting thing for students to attend

Planning Lock-Ins on a Shoestring Budget

I'm tempted to just say, "Go back and read the first 22 chapters for basic tips," but the following is a short list of ideas taken from all the chapters of this book.

Space

Do you have rooms at the church that you don't typically use for youth ministry? What if you borrowed additional rooms at church for the night and converted them into "boutique" rooms? How about a dedicated video game space or a nail spa salon room? Don't underestimate how cool the sanctuary or hallways can be for giant games of tag.

Technology

There are so many ideas you could employ here! How about setting up a computer as a photo booth and giving students hours to take funny pictures of themselves? You could also find LCD projectors around the church and play video games on giant screens or white walls.

Money

Are there any donors at the church who might have resources available for a "missions-focused outreach" instead of just doing a lock-in? How about charging a little more on a fall retreat and rolling leftover funds into a lock-in? An extra $20 per person for a fall retreat might not seem much, but having those extra funds available for a lock-in (that kids view as costing them nothing) might be great.

Transportation/Vehicles

Safety is a priority, but also consider renting school buses instead of charter buses. Or maybe you have a transportation company in town that wants to donate bus time. Don't forget about parents driving or even your young adult group; you also could have a Sunday school class commit to driving for an event as a monthly outreach.

Community/City Resources

Does your city have a parks department or someone who runs sports leagues? Chances are these officials might have recreation degrees and are full of ideas that could help you. Asking for city-employee help is sometimes important. What if you want to light a bonfire? Is it legal? A great ending to a crud war is a fire truck at the event as the firefighters hose down kids who're covered in goo.

Often communities have gyms, parks, pools, etc., that you should look at. It's significantly cheaper to rent a city gym or park and plan an event there than it is to use a "fun zone"! It might be that just going to a different location for a while, away from the church, makes a big difference all by itself. (And if you've never taken kids ice-blocking—which involves using blocks of ice as sleds when there's no snow—using a community space is definitely something you should consider.)

Dumpster Diving, Garage Sales, Thrift Stores, and Hardware Stores

Dumpster diving isn't always legal, but being on the lookout for discarded items you might be able to use always is. Think about how you could create a huge maze with giant boxes from a refrigerator store; or how about getting a bunch of old suits from a thrift store for a costume party or giving students scissors so they can make new outfits (as with the *Design Star* TV show)? Hardware stores are also a bit of a dream place. You never know what you might find that can help you dream up fun ideas for a lock-in.

Network

Are there other youth workers in your town who might have great ideas for you? What about partnering with another church and using both of your spaces and resources? How about bringing in a friend from another church to speak?

People in the Congregation

Don't forget to *actually ask* folks from the congregation to help you run the lock-in! You might not find any long-term volunteers among them, but what if you just needed someone to come make hamburgers? Or what if someone who works in a nail salon is willing to host that area of the lock-in? You might be surprised at the resources you have available to you just through the skills and gifts of people sitting in your pews.

Friends and Family

Do you have any local friends who could help you staff an event? What about asking parents to drive, hang out with kids, or just make a ton of cookies?

Parachurch Ministries

Young Life does an amazing job reaching out to students who don't generally come to church. What about partnering with YL to do an outreach event? Or do they have relationships with other organizations that you could benefit from later on?

Camps, Colleges, Seminaries

Are any of these spots available as a site for your event? You might find a camp or college or seminary with great space and—depending on when you're scheduling your event—such spots may be empty. You also could get some great volunteers through camps, colleges, and seminaries. Or you could think even bigger: What about finding an intern from one of these entities to pull off the whole thing?

Training Organizations

Look into Youth Specialties, Group, the Red Cross, YMCA, etc., and how they can help you. Make parents happy and have EMTs or other medical staff at your event. YS has a ton of books as well as a network of people who can come in and host. Our local YMCA hosts a volleyball league at our church and has told us we can use its facility.

Denominational Help

Again, are there other churches in your denomination that might want to partner with you or allow you to use its space or resources? Can you trade resources with another church?

Other Church Ministries

Again, always ask. There may be Sunday school classes that would want to take on this event as a project.

History

Have you done this before? Maybe the church has a long history of this event and promoting it will be easy. Also look to people who've done this kind of thing before to ask them how it went. What can you learn from them?

Longevity/Relational Equity

If you've been around a while, you probably have some favors you can call in. Maybe there are some church families who can loan you their properties (e.g., lake house or cabin)? Build relationships and know that people often will help if you ask.

Failures/Successes

I recommend always taking notes after an event so you have a written record of what worked and what didn't. Use those notes as you plan future events. Ask other youth workers what has worked for them (and hasn't worked). Who's pulled off a successful lock-in?

Dreams and Aspirations

How great do you want this to be? What are your dreams for it? A big resource for you will end up being *your desire* to make this event as great as you want it to be. If your expectations are low, then chances are the event won't be very successful.

Education

Did you take any recreation classes? Youth ministry courses? Good! Then pull out your old notes, textbooks, and articles. What have you learned from those times in the classroom that can help you with an all-nighter? You probably pulled a few all-nighters in college. What made them work? Were they fun?

Culture

Before you decide to do a lock-in, ask questions about your community and the culture of the church. Is this event something you're trying to shoehorn into a culture that doesn't value it? Do you have an expectation in your culture or community that this is what youth ministries do?

chapter 24

Retreats/Camps on a Shoestring

CAMPS AND RETREATS have always been a mainstay of youth ministry. Most youth workers at some point have said to parents, "If your sons and daughters attend this weekend retreat, we'll spend more time with them than if they came to every single Sunday morning worship service for an entire school year."

Such a statement may not be completely accurate in terms of timeline, but it does reflect the belief among youth workers that extended periods of time with students is always a good thing.

If you work at a church without much money budgeted to the youth ministry, and if your students don't have the funds to pay the costs for attending camps and retreats, it's tough to even think about doing them.

Hopefully some of these tips will get you off the ground and running. (You may not want to implement all of these tips at the same time, but strategically using your resources and saving money where you can is a good start.)

Some Camp/Retreat Shoestring Tips

Space

Get it free. Borrow a youth room from another church, a family cabin, lake house, ranch, camp site, RV, boat, or anywhere else you can get kids to sleep. Housing on retreats is generally one of the most expensive costs.

Technology

What do you need that you can borrow or beg for? Students are pretty savvy in this area, and sometimes you can pull off some great activities and crowdbreakers with, for instance, a Wii hooked up to a borrowed projection unit pointed at a big white wall. Can't get a Wii? Okay—you can probably borrow an older game system. You'll be amazed at how much kids still love to play those things. What if you had a karaoke or music video creation room? Borrow a Mac with Garage Band and see what kind of songs they can make up. There are so many ways you can use technology to spice up a retreat!

Money

Find food coupons or research new locations and activities. See if you can talk a group at your church into sponsoring a meal. Get a local business to put its logo on T-shirts and make them for you (free). See what kinds of donations you can get from local stores. For families who can't afford the camp or retreat, offer to put them on payment plans. Be creative regarding where you spend money and how you spend it.

Transportation/Vehicles

This depends on the distance you need to travel. Do everything you can to *avoid renting vehicles*. Instead try to get church members to donate their time by driving *their* vehicles. See if parents can drop off and pick up at the camp location. Carpool. Partner with another church that may have transportation available. Split costs. If you have to rent, ask for discounts. See if your nonprofit church status can free you from paying taxes. Ask about packages and multiple-trip discounts.

Community/City Resources

Maybe you don't even have to leave the neighborhood to pull off a retreat. Does your city have any interesting spaces or resources you can use? Creativity is key.

Dumpster Diving, Garage Sales, Thrift Stores, Hardware Stores

One thing that often makes a retreat or camp fun is activities. What things can you "find" that you can repurpose to launch a fun activity?

We once did an amazing relay race with random stuff at each location; students had to build the craziest contraption to win. Running from place to place they took duct tape and just kept building. (The coolest part? Junk from dumpsters can go right back into them after you're done. Someone's junk may be your greatest resource!)

Network

Ask someone in your youth ministry network to come speak for free. Do a swap so next time you speak at your colleague's camp. Same thing if you need a musician. Ask your network for what you need. If you need a portable sound system chances are someone has one. Maybe someone with a bus at another church would be willing to drive you to camp. This is potentially the area where you can find the most shoestring help if you've spent the time building a solid network.

Congregation

Again, it sounds simple, but what if you simply asked your congregation to help? If it's an occasional thing where you've sold the vision on why you are doing the camp or retreat, you might find some great help. What if an adult Sunday school class came along and prepared all the food? What if they provided transportation or just baked cookies? Everything helps.

Friends and Families

We try to get parents involved in all that we do. In general they like to come and be a part of our retreats. They know all the other parents and can be a huge advocate for your needs. Get your friends involved, too. You've probably got some pretty great friends who would occasionally like to help you do what you do.

Parachurch Ministries

Just as with your youth ministry network, these folks are amazing people. See how you can partner with them. I note earlier that we've shared our youth ministry space for free over the years with a few parachurch ministries in our area—but "free" doesn't always mean without obligations. Just set it up beforehand and say something like "I might ask you once every couple of years to speak at a camp in exchange for using the room."

Camps, Colleges, Seminaries

Don't forget about dorms. Colleges often have great spots to conduct retreats during the summer because most of their students are on vacation, there's plenty of wide-open space, and the colleges would love to fill that space. Dorms are cheaper than hotels and nicer than sleeping on a church floor. Also you may have some staff from those places who'd love to help for cheap.

Training Organizations

We used to conduct some "water trips" every year, and I always tried to bring an EMT, nurse, or doctor with us on each one. We used contacts at the YMCA and Red Cross and just asked them if they had anyone who'd be willing to come for free.

Youth Ministry Training

One resource I've seen used over the years is the great content on the Youth Specialties Web site. One thing they do that I love—every year after the National Youth Workers Convention, YS posts all their videos, banners, and slides and makes them free downloads. So if you're looking for a great winter camp theme, just wait until early December and then download a whole package of visuals. You'll look slick, and it's free.

History

Especially if you're new to the church, check with people who've been around for a long time and see what resources they've used in the past. You might find that they already have some amazing shoestring-type ideas.

Closing
Thoughts

I NOTE THIS EARLIER, but it bears repeating here: This book isn't built on an "ideas book" model. So if you want to do a retreat and turn to a relevant page, you won't find a step-by-step process all laid out for you. The shoestring approach doesn't work that way. To truly figure out how youth ministry on a shoestring works, you have to approach it with big open eyes to the resources available to you and see how those resources work in your context to create activities.

Many of you might feel as though you have practically zero resources. You just want to pull something off but don't know where to start. My advice is to start networking and talking to other youth workers. See what they're doing and how they're doing it. Also take the first three sections of this book and use the space provided after each chapter to take notes and begin thinking about what resources you *do* have available. You might be surprised by how much you actually have at your disposal that you never knew about. Always start your planning with a look at resources. In my opinion this is a healthier way to plan and think about what you can do.

Some of you work for churches that have experienced severe budget cuts—and money to the youth ministry was the first line item to go. But perhaps you have a history of doing camps, retreats, activities, and mission trips, and you want to keep doing them despite the lack of needed funds. The ideas here will help you.

This was my story. I'm at a pretty big church. We've historically had a whole bunch of resources at our disposal, but in the last few years our budgets have been slashed big time. We've wanted to keep doing the things we'd been doing, so we've had to figure out ways of maximizing resources and doing more for less.

The economy may turn around, and perhaps one day soon we'll all have larger budgets. But regardless of what happens economically, I believe that the shoestring ideas in these pages will always be worth using. Why? Because doing more for less in one area allows you to do more in other areas.

Other Shoestring Stories

As the following pages demonstrate, there are a ton of great people out there with wonderful ideas—and sometimes just asking them for their ideas will turn out to be our biggest help.

The Reagan Casket, Etc.

I was in the basement of my church wandering around, looking for something—anything—useful. I found a wooden stage about 10 feet long and 4 feet wide. It looked like the perfect size for a mini stage, and I started thinking about how we could throw that in the back of a truck when we had events and always have a stage with us. I started dreaming about having a second stage in the youth room. Then our facilities guy pulled me back into reality: No, I couldn't have the stage because that's where the coffin of former U.S. president Ronald Reagan sat while his body "laid in state" at the church! Small world. So, no, I didn't get my portable stage. But at least I asked. You'll never get resources if you don't ask.

Some of my best interactions with students have been as direct results of not having the financial resources to buy what I wanted. Because I couldn't just cut a check or put it on a credit card, my staff and I had to think long and hard about what we really wanted to accomplish, what resources (besides money) I could tap into, and where the money we did have could be better spent. This more intentional thinking helped us be more committed and intentional about the environments and interactions we programmed.

I do lots of experiential activities, and the props to pull off these activities can be expensive if you buy them premade from the resource companies. I have found great materials at stores such as Target, Ikea, and Home Depot. If you see or read about an activity you'd like to do, take a walk through one of these stores and look at the materials with your activity in mind. You'll see things differently.

I made a $50 marble tube activity set for $10 in wall molding and three marbles (borrowed from a small child). PVC pipe is great for simple, cheap set design and activity materials. I made an outdoor projection screen for $25 with PVC pipes and connectors and a king-size bedsheet. I also made a giant tossing game with PVC, plastic gallon jugs of water, and some donated nylons.

—*John Losey*
Director/Owner, Praxis Training (praxistraining.com),
Youth Worker

The Pros and Cons of Outside Voices

When thinking about training or consulting on a shoestring, two things come to mind. On one hand, church leaders are too quick to look for outside help. Our infatuation with experts, leaders, and authors, combined with our belief that there's a "right way" to do youth ministry, is a dangerous combination. This leads us to spending money excessively on the hopes that experts who've never set foot in our churches will help us discover the solutions for our youth ministries! One even could say that we don't believe God has given us everything we need to face the situations that come our way. It's helpful to check our motives when it comes to training, and often it's best to simply save money rather than chase after another expert with another model.

On the other hand, unique voices from outside our communities can help us uncover dormant potential—or they may affirm our direction. The power of consultants is that they know your context, they speak the truth about your reality, and they can affirm the real potential within your particular community. While it may be difficult to put a price tag on that kind of perspective, spending anywhere from $3,000 to even $20,000 on consulting might seem insane when you minister on a shoestring. Then again, gaining a unique perspective saves most churches five or more years in time, youth ministry budget, and salary—which saves the average church more than $100,000. Certainly I'm biased on the subject, and consulting has pitfalls. Either way, let's stop looking for the expert to save us and continue to trust that God has given us what we need as a community.

—*Mark Riddle*
The Riddle Group

The ONE Network

It was born several years ago when, after a See You at the Pole event, we recognized that most youth workers in town were there and someone said, "Hey! Let's get breakfast and hang out!" A few hours later, our discussion made us realize that about a third of the high school and middle schoolers in our area were attending our churches regularly. The thought of unifying around our similarities instead of our differences and becoming allies instead of adversaries took root. The thought of bringing our students together as ONE would change the face of the schools, and as a result could change the face of the community and surrounding areas. We began with a couple of corporate worship events that led to other events and retreats together. We crafted a ONE statement for members to agree with based on Scripture, and we saw students and the community respond. The ONE Network has continued to evolve and now partners directly with the school district.

When tragedies happen in the teenage community, we're invited to counsel and console students on campus. We have guest lectured for teachers about family and marriage. We were invited to (and taught) a weeklong national elective on abstinence. Because of our relationships with the school district, it's developing a program called "Connect" to help kids and families further bond with faith-based organizations in the community—and the school district is recommending kids and families who need it most to the local churches! Also teachers have asked us for "work" that their students can do for free, including photography, graphic design, and video editing. We've created internships for those students, and the results are incredible. We've also provided a work environment for special-needs students.

The students in our youth ministries are still learning what it means to band together as we model it for them, and it has started to trickle up to some of our church's senior pastors and other leaders. The best part of all of this is I only budget $500 a year for the ONE network.

—Charlie Hellmuth
Youth Pastor
First Baptist of Coppell, Texas

Just Ask

Jesus wasn't joking when he said, "Ask and it will be given to you" (Luke 11:9). Now this may not have been exactly what he was thinking about, but in my experience with youth ministry on a small budget, I've found that one of the easiest things you can do is simply ask people for what you need.

When I was doing youth ministry in a small rural church in Idaho, I emailed a lot of Christian music labels and asked if they could provide free music for our youth to check out. I was overwhelmed with the response. I received packages for the next few months that included CDs, DVDs, posters to decorate our youth room, and even complimentary tickets to concerts that were coming through our area.

In my current church, I've found that we had quite a few youth who were really gifted in the area of video editing, but we didn't have a digital camcorder. So I jumped online and emailed the PR/marketing departments of some electronics companies, shared with them some of the creative ways our youth would be using their products, and within a few weeks, I received three different high-end HD handheld camcorders that our youth now use for video contests and other things in our youth ministry.

Could our youth ministries have survived without the gifts we received? Sure. They weren't necessities. But they helped get kids excited about various aspects of our group, and they thought it was pretty cool that people from these companies were so generous to offer these gifts to them.

I believe people are more generous than we often assume they will be. This goes for individuals in our churches, too. So, why not ask?

If someone says no, you haven't lost anything. But you'd be surprised what's available out there if you just ask.

—*Adam Walker Cleaveland*
pomomusings.com

Collaborate!

The large majority of my youth ministry experience has been in small church settings where big budgets and large numbers of resources are rarely available. One of the best ways I kept it cheap and simple was by collaborating with other small church youth ministry departments. I tag-teamed with three youth pastors, and we did an event together. This event collaboration had many advantages: We shouldered the cost together, brought kids together, built and unified relationships with other churches, and networked with other local youth ministries.

The best collaboration event I did was an overnight broomball tournament with three local youth ministries. All three met at the ice rink at 1 a.m., and we played broomball for three hours. Each group brought food to share. The students loved it, and more importantly our church budget loved it: For $10 each, students played broomball for three hours and ate unlimited snacks and drinks.

Collaboration and networking can go a long way for small church youth ministries with limited resources.

—*Jeremy Zach*
Orange XP3 Specialist

T.E.A.M. (Together Everyone Achieves More)

It may sound like a cliché, but it is true: We can do more together than we can separately. I've served at churches of different sizes—from 90 to 900—with even more diverse budgets. At each church I was near a megachurch with a seemingly unlimited budget and thousands of youth. It seemed I could never do the cool events I saw other churches doing because I lacked people and funds. Then it finally occurred to me that I could do these things through collaboration.

So I immediately went to some of my trusted co-laborers in youth ministry. The first thing they suggested was a combined winter retreat. I had wanted to do a winter retreat for several years but couldn't justify the cost of taking only a few students. I considered taking them to a camp-style winter retreat, but I wanted to have some say in regard to the look, feel, and message of the weekend. Combining with two youth ministry colleagues allowed me the influence I wanted as well as the numbers and shared responsibility I needed. Our three churches brought 75 youth together for a wonderful weekend. The costs were kept at bay by sharing the fees, the speaking was solid as we split up the teaching sessions, the small groups were fresh because we distributed people evenly, and everyone had fun meeting new people. It was a success on every level.

Since then I've collaborated on every kind of event you can think of. Worship services, concerts (that really helps defray costs), retreats, mission trips, service projects, mentoring, and many other things. Admittedly not every collaboration event matched the success of that first winter retreat. But every time has been a model of the body of Christ. When we come together intentionally we reflect the body image Paul uses in 1 Corinthians.

I'm careful, however, about what I collaborate on and who I collaborate with. I look at each event and potential collaborator carefully: For some activities I don't wish to collaborate with certain churches (i.e., if our doctrine differs too much). If you're trying to do youth ministry on a shoestring, give collaboration a try. I've saved a ton of money, met a bunch of great people, and was part of being a living example of the body of Christ.

—*Aaron Geisler*
Associate Pastor of Youth and Children

What You Don't Know Can Hurt You

You've probably heard people say, "What you don't know can't hurt you!" Well, I'm not so sure that's true. My observation is that much of what youth ministers don't know ends up hurting them. I'm the executive director of the Center for Youth Ministry Training, and I work with youth ministers in their first three years. The following are a few things our young youth ministers "don't know" that often hurt them:

- Youth ministers spend more time on planning, administration, and training others than with youth.
- Letting youth drive your car is a bad idea.
- Parents are more important to their children's faith than youth workers are.
- Equipping volunteers will grow the ministry faster and more effectively than you can by yourself.
- Churches are hard places to work.
- Having medical releases is important prior to kids running through glass walls or the other mistakes you can find at failblog.ymblogs.com.

A worse danger is "what you don't know might hurt someone else." Teenagers are fickle creatures. I once said something that led a kid to stop coming to church and didn't find out about it until four years later. Many a youth ministry exists that's built on the theological sand of games, fun, and Jesus "Lite" instead of a theological foundation that stands the tests of this world.

We are responsible for what we know and don't know as leaders; therefore seeking training that equips us with skills and knowledge is essential to leading well. What are your strengths and weaknesses as a youth minister? Take the time to look for training that will help you lead from your strengths while creating support for your weaknesses. You'll end up knowing more, which (in theory at least) allows fewer things to hurt you.

—Dietrich "Deech" Kirk
Center for Youth Ministry Training (www.cymt.org)

Creative Camping

Camps have been a cornerstone of youth ministry for a very long time. They are also big-ticket items. I work at a small church with no budget. To compound this problem my small church has a youth group filled with kids from families who can't afford several hundred dollars to send their students away for a weekend. Over the years I've had to come up with ideas to supplement camp funding. Here are three things we have done:

First, I teamed up with other churches in my area. One year five churches in my denomination grouped together and rented a camp. By staffing it ourselves we saved a lot of money. We also agreed that the churches that could afford to charge more per student would do so in order to allow the smaller churches to come.

Second, I stayed close to home. By changing the event from "camp" to a "retreat" you have some flexibility regarding where you go. The expectation isn't necessarily cabins and campfires.

Third, rely on your contacts. Design a weekend around what you have. If you know someone with a boat, go get wet. If you know someone with a beach house, sounds like it's about time for a surf trip. But it's not so much where you're going; it's the mechanics of the trip. For example, meals can be a big cost at camp. Invite church members to buy and cook one meal for the group. If you can get five groups of church members to do that, you've probably cut the cost of your weekend by $30 per student.

—*David Derus*
Youth Worker

Meaningful Experiences without a Huge Price Tag

I believe that students (all people for that matter) long for meaningful experiences and personal encounters with God. These moments change and transform us. They provide vision and calling for our futures. They remind us that we were made for relationship with God.

The great thing about these encounters is that they don't cost anything. The moments that bear the most fruit in ministry don't require large budgets; they only require intentionality on our part to create sacred spaces conducive to these sorts of encounters. This requires a shift in our thinking and ministry philosophy away from events and recreational incentives and toward moments where we're stretched, uncomfortable, and free from distraction.

One of my favorite things to do with students is take them backpacking. While this might seem daunting at first, usually you can find someone in your church with experience who can act as an informal guide, and often the equipment can be found in the garages of many of your church members. Costs for the trip end up being for food and gas.

Besides the physical challenge, what I like about backpacking is that it involves going somewhere remote, away from where you're comfortable, to a place that's quiet and beautiful. In short, you enter a perfect opportunity to meet God. Taking a journal and Bible along, students have the opportunity to be spoken to in true "surround sound." We hear God's voice not just through the Word but in the unfamiliar silence, in the beauty of creation, and in the quiet, uninterrupted times of reflection. Youth leaders need not provide any additional content; they just need to facilitate the experience. Direct teens to God's voice and help them hear his whisper that's otherwise drowned out by our world of hurry, pressure, and stimulation.

Not only will this equip them to recognize God's voice at home, it will provide them with an encounter they won't easily forget—and one that will stretch your budget much further than a snowboarding weekend or a week at an expensive camp.

—Jeff Tacklind
Pastor of Teaching
Laguna (CA) Church by the Sea

If You Don't Ask, You'll Never Know!

These words were shared by a professor in a negotiation class I took in graduate school. Actually his words led up to one of the most creative and fun (yes, I use those two words in conjunction with academics) assignments I ever received in graduate school: *Negotiate better deals before our next class.* The prof added, "If you don't ask for a better deal, you will never know if a better deal is possible." I did the assignment, and it worked (e.g., I received two cups of coffee for the price of one—because I asked)!

The point of the assignment was not to learn how to manipulate people but to discover how many consumer situations are negotiable. I continue to practice this philosophy in my student ministry—it works!

I've practiced student ministry with little or no budget and with grand amounts of money, and frugality has been a priority in both plenty and little—it's good for both the church and family/student budgets. In other words, the "if you don't ask, you'll never know" principle has received a good workout. Allow me to offer my fellow frugal youth workers (and yet-to-be-frugal youth workers) a short list of some of the places where you should ask for better deals—the places that have said yes to me:

Grocery Stores

Ask grocery stores if they're willing to give you a deal or donate food for a retreat, camp, service project, or fundraiser.

Large Megastore Chains

The larger chains have the ability to cut better deals and often have programs that assist with youth-type organizations. Get to know your local megastore managers and see if they can offer you any deals and/or donations on food, supplies, clothes, etc.

Fast-Food Chains

You can build great relationships with fast-food chains (especially if you always leave the place clean when you leave). Oh, and did you know that many fast-food chains offer free meals to van and bus drivers?

School Administrators, Coaches, Teachers, Etc.

These individuals often have the authority to permit outside youth group access to athletic fields, gyms, and *cafetoriums* (one of my favorite words).

Starving Artists, Speakers, and/or Entertainers

Many of these people and groups need venues to further their careers and will play/entertain for the exposure and ability to sell product.

Up-and-Coming Artists, Speakers, and Entertainers

Not at the top of the heap yet, but fast approaching. In other words, they're still affordable. Hint: When you go to national conferences, pay attention to the sampled artists, speakers, and entertainers and begin to negotiate show dates and fees at their merch tables.

Skilled Craftspeople at Your Church

These individuals can transform spaces at little or no (if they donate the materials) cost. If they are business owners, they can even provide trailers for luggage transport and work deals for service project supplies.

Snack Vendors in Your Church

These individuals often have more snacks than they can stock and sell. These items have a date stamp and have to go somewhere.

Any Service Industry

Airlines, hotels, and restaurants can offer deals because of the volume of business you're providing. If you're a smaller ministry, don't give up on the benefit of "volume" discounts.

Christian Colleges

Many will let you stay in their dorms and even offer discounted food if you let them talk up their campus to your students. They can also provide artists, speakers, camp counselors, and entertainers in exchange for the opportunity to rub shoulders with your students and parents. This is a very competitive market that can really bless your ministry with resources.

Have fun practicing the "if you don't ask, you'll never know" principle as you save money for your ministry. Oh . . . and one important piece of advice on negotiating: Always be courteous and respectful when asking for the better deal!

—*David Fraze*

Create Space for Family Play

Being from Los Angeles, I notice that parents and their kids spend most of their lives together in cars traveling from one destination to the next. Everything is on the go. Eating. Homework. Conversations. Life. With everyone being so busy and going in so many different directions (and that's just within the family unit!), no one has time to stop and enjoy time together.

One of the things we've tried to create is space for parents and kids to play together. Once a semester we do a "Family Game Night" which includes board games, video games, and active games such as dodge ball and Capture the Flag.

Another event we recently adopted (that I could not believe people liked) was kickball. When I was looking for ideas from area youth pastors, one of them said kickball was a huge success. I couldn't believe how fun this event was for our families, and it was so simple.

One thing about these events is that we try to hold them during "non-meal" times. It seems a lot less intimidating for families to bring a snack as opposed to a portion of a meal. Parents love to bring snacks to these types of events, which makes the event super cheap, too. Along with the simplicity of the games we play, it makes for a fun and communal time together.

—*R.O. Smith*
Codirector of Student Discipleship
Bel Air (CA) Presbyterian Church

Asking Isn't Stealing

How do you start an inner-city youth ministry from scratch with no budget? You ask for help!

That's exactly how our ministry began. We had no staff, no budget, no building, and zero resources. But while we were resource poor, we were vision rich. Our mindset was that asking wasn't stealing. If our vision was true, God would confirm it as members of our community embraced it.

The problems were big and obvious. First, we didn't have a place to meet. We're part of a church plant which rents a local high school's auditorium on Sunday morning, so we knew we couldn't meet there for our midweek program. And while several people were open to the idea of meeting in their homes, San Diego houses tend to be too small to contain 25 teenagers. Fortunately a nearby church gave us unlimited use of their building on Tuesday evenings. All we did was share the vision of what we were trying to do and why we thought their building would help us, and within minutes we had a set of keys and a code to the alarm system.

As we began, one of our values was to become a Christian family for students who didn't have one. We knew that the easiest way to express that value was by offering a weekly meal to our students. But the fact that we didn't have a kitchen or a volunteer to cook or a budget to buy food hardly fazed us; when we shared our vision with a local restaurant owner, he agreed to provide the main ingredients of our weekly meal. So each Tuesday night we meet in a borrowed church building and eat free burritos from a local business.

Then, like most other youth groups, we knew that a winter retreat would be perfect for going deep with our students. Of course, we had absolutely no budget and no way to raise enough money for every student to attend. So we started asking around and found a church about 45 minutes outside of town in a beautiful mountain community that let us use their youth building for the weekend for free. Again, all it took was us sharing our ministry vision and asking with an attitude of "asking isn't stealing."

Our youth ministry has found amazing richness in having no budget.

—*Adam McLane*
All Things Social
Youth Specialties

Redefining Resources

What do you do when your youth ministry's budget is reduced by 75 percent over a five-year span but the size of your community grows during the same time?

It happened to us, so we've learned to redefine *resources* so we could re-source our ministry.

We'd always defined *resources* as budget, buildings, and staff. With budgets (and staff) getting slashed, we had to add another category to our resource inventory: people. Now I know "people" often get lumped into the staff category, but I'm talking about much more than staff; I'm talking about anybody who cares about youth, whether paid staff, volunteer staff, church member, nonmember . . . even non-Christian! By cultivating a relational network of community members who care about youth, we've been able to re-source our ministry with these new resources.

For example, one of the dads in our high school ministry approached us about wanting to start an outreach surf ministry. Looking at our budget, buildings, and staff, there was no way we could launch a surf ministry among all the other things we were doing—but there was a huge need based on our local surfing population. We didn't believe our resources could support the need, but here he was—passionate, excited, and willing to spearhead it. So we let him run with it.

In two months pro surfer Tim Curran donated surfboards, local surf shops donated two rolling racks of wetsuits, and volunteers came out of the woodwork to help teach kids how to surf. Water bottles were delivered, a Web site was built, and surf wax was packaged with our ministry name on it . . . all for free!

It's been four years since the surf ministry started, and it's still going strong as hundreds have learned how to surf, Bible studies have been launched, and a team even traveled to Costa Rica to partner with Christian Surfers International to build a community park and teach kids how to surf in Jaco, one of the epicenters for prostitution in Central America.

And all of this happened because we re-sourced our ministry through one of the greatest resources we didn't even know we had: people.

—*Drew Sams*
Pastor of Student Ministries
Calvary Community Church, Westlake Village, CA

Social Media

There is, perhaps, no better source for free event planning than the social media bonanza offered today. These tools are not merely great sources of information; they're also the means by which you can tell the stories about the personality of your group: your convictions, thoughts, questions, and certainly your sense of humor.

Of course it all starts with Facebook. Almost everyone is there and checks in regularly (unlike email or voice mail). Make sure your group has a Facebook page with meeting times, places, and a schedule of upcoming events. Create an event page for every special event and encourage your group members to share, share, share.

In addition to Facebook, social media allows for you to tell your stories in myriad ways. Set up a YouTube channel for your group and post regular goings-on and things that reflect your group's personality. Many phones now allow you not only to shoot video but edit on the fly and post directly to your channel. And who knows? You could even be the source of one of those legendary Internet sensations!

An example: Exodus—the senior high ministry of First Baptist Church of Stockton, California—is responsible for the 2010 YouTube hit, "Cats Playing Patty-cake, what they were saying . . ." (http://www.youtube.com/watch?v=X3iFhLdWjqc). At the time of this writing, the clip received more than three million views in its first three weeks. It's simple, bizarre, funny, and likely represents the personalities of the members of the group. There is no link to the group's site, no proselytizing, just the clip with slides at the beginning and end. Many comments in those three weeks simply thank the group for a funny video. What better way to invite people to join you than to show how warm and funny your group is?

The same goes for other media, and it can mean that you don't have to create everything for the group. The following are a few examples:

- Photos. A Flickr account lets you document all your activities and invite others to join in.
- Writing. Have your group members contribute their blog posts and open up the content for your site. Post reviews of music, movies, television shows, or books that are part of your group's everyday discourse.

These opportunities also allow you to engage teens in the things that interest them. In addition to photography, videography, writing, and graphic design are huge among teens. And while monetarily free, it's not cheap. In other words, this is your public face—a place where trust is initiated and developed. Telling great stories—and allowing your teens to be a part of telling them—is a powerful message about who you are and what you value.

—Dave Palmer
www.dunktankmarketing.com

"Money Talks"

Sure, it's a well-known statement. And too often it's true. Want to get something done? Money can make it happen. Want something to be successful? Find the funding. We're pretty convinced, whether it's rational or just in our bones, that money can solve almost any problem. So not surprisingly we typically believe that a little money (or preferably a lot) wired into our youth ministry budget will go a long way toward transforming our dented and rusted ministries into shiny and new ministries.

Yet the biblical story says nothing about money talking. Money is real; economics is no doubt a principality and reality. But the confession of the church, of Israel, of Jesus himself, is that *God speaks*—not money. The Christian faith is a faith of Word; a Word spoken, not just by human beings, but by God's very self. The church is the community that seeks to hear this Word and respond to it. And there's no down payment needed to encounter this Word. In fact, it often comes to those with empty pockets and outstanding debts, to the poor and the broken.

If this is true, then at its core youth ministry can't be about big shiny programs that are so often contingent upon money—on making money talk—that shouts at kids to participate and believe. At its core, ministry is about the confession to and participation with a God who speaks, who speaks life out of death, being out of nonbeing.

So ministry is about inviting young people to encounter this Word. But I guess this is where money comes into play. We need to use money (big programs and extravagant events) to get kids close enough to the church so they can hear this Word, right?

No, I actually believe that encountering the Word, the speaking of God, happens not through the events themselves but rather through encountering the people there. The Word becomes flesh in the humanity of Jesus; God speaks fully and completely in the very life, death, and resurrection of Jesus. This means, then, that we encounter the Word of God in our shared humanity; we find God with and for young people (Matthew 25).

I've argued in other places that, at its core, ministry (youth or otherwise) is about seeking the presence of God in and through our relationships (see *Relationships Unfiltered*). And this takes a very small budget; it can be done on a shoestring. But what it does take is something much richer: people who want the Word that God speaks right alongside the humanity of teenagers; people who want to be in relationship with youth as a way of encountering the Word that truly speaks, offering life out of death.

—*Andrew Root, Ph.D.*
Associate Professor Youth and Family Ministry
Luther Seminary

It's All about Relationships

We didn't have a church building. My office was a backpack, and our supplies lived in a box in my car. Our youth group met in the parking lot and storage room of a woodworking business. Yet even lacking all the apparent "necessities" for youth ministry, we met weekly, laughed a lot, and were led by the Holy Spirit to grow in faith. We were far from a wealthy church, but we had a lot of heart, creativity, and adults who shared whatever they had. That youth group was filled with a number of students whose positive attitudes were absolutely contagious.

One activity in particular became a bonding and unifying time for the entire church. Not far from our "church" was a park. At this park, the church held an annual youth versus adults kickball game. The total cost of this church-wide event: $10 (and only another $10 if we "overused" the ball during the previous game). The entire church staff bought into this event, and that was a key. We declared it "casual Sunday" and encouraged everyone to attend whether they planned on playing or not. Everyone brought picnic lunches that turned into an amazing potluck as people shared what they brought—and those who were unable to bring anything always had plenty to eat. We had our own time of loaves and fishes. Then the game followed. Only a handful of adults attending would (or actually could) play, but the others cheered—and heckled as the case may be. Students came out for the afternoon and gave it their all. Even with competition being fierce and the winning team retaining bragging rights until the next match, everyone left with a strong sense of community and new stories to share.

The game was the reason to gather; the relationships we were building were the reason to continue. Through this one simple event, multiple generations spent the day together. We began in church together, shared a meal, then laughed and played throughout the day. Names were learned, conversations took place, and connections were made. Our corporate times of prayer throughout the year were strengthened because we knew each other. It was evident in this one simple activity that God worked through a game and an almost free activity to build his kingdom in ways we never imagined or anticipated.

—*Amy Jacober, Ph.D.*
Associate Professor of Practical Theology and Youth Ministry
Truett Theological Seminary

Train Your Staff with a Therapist/Counselor

Youth ministry is an amazing profession, but with it comes all kinds of often-overlooked issues in the ministry world. Issues such as establishing healthy boundaries, self-care, avoiding burnout, and understanding how to deal with various pastoral care issues that often arise when working with students.

When it's possible I believe most youth pastors would like to receive extra training for themselves and their youth staff. But how does one go about providing and receiving extra training when the budget is tight, when there's little to no money available to make it happen?

Bring in a professional therapist/counselor to provide the necessary training for yourself or the staff. This collaboration can become the perfect partnership, as many youth pastors need or seek counselors/therapists to help guide them with pastoral care issues, and many therapists/counselors rely on referrals from youth pastors.

Here are some suggestions:

- If you don't already have a relationship with a counselor/therapist, do some research and find out who's a trusted voice in your community or church.
- Discuss with the counselor/therapist some topics you believe you or your staff would like more training on (e.g., self-care, setting healthy boundaries, avoiding burnout, mandated reporting issues, as well as suicide, cutting, sexuality, etc.).
- If you believe this counselor/therapist is a good fit, ask him or her to come in and speak.
- Some counselors will charge their hourly rate to present, but some will do it free because they know the referral benefits of connections with youth ministry.
- If you learn from the training, set up a quarterly training seminar for your staff.

This is just one way that a youth ministry can cut costs and still provide top-notch service for themselves and others.

—*Rhett Smith (M.Div., MSMFT)*
Marriage and Family Therapist

Low Cost, High Impact

"I want the best!"

This should be the mantra of every youth worker for everything; budget should be a minor consideration. Why? Because the best things in life are free, and networking is where "best" meets "free," where low cost meets high impact. Networking is one of the best things a leader can do, period. Not only is it great strategy, but it's what Christ wants from us as his followers. Plus it's very cost effective.

Networking Is a Great Return on Investment

Every leader wants the best bang for the buck, the best use of their time. Networking has a way of creating synergy that other things don't. Working a couple of hours on a project is a great way to check off items on a to-do list; but networking for a few hours is the start of connectivity, brand-building, and kingdom impact. Working alone is like counting the seeds in an apple; networking is like counting the apples in a seed.

Relationships Are the Resource

I'm convinced that everything great in life happens through relationships. God, spouse, kids, family, friends—life's most important commodities are all people. The very essence of the gospel is people: God loves people; people need help. Jesus sacrificed to help people; we need to do the same. If people are such a high priority to God, they should be to all of his followers as well.

People Are Our Greatest Assets

At the end of the day we're in the people business; programs and papers pale in comparison. If we build people, we win. And while networking with other youth workers is important, it's easily set aside. We need to see ourselves as relationship brokers who deal in human capital.

Reciprocity

Pay It Forward is not only a movie title; it's also a biblical truth. Everyone has something to give and something to learn; we should do it together. We're better together.

I'm convinced that networking is the single best thing a leader can do, but it's also the easiest thing to cross off a crowded to-do list. If we could truly see the value of giving and receiving, of the practical and spiritual nature of networking, it would become a resource we could not be without.

—*Rawd Jones*
Pure Group
Dallas Networking

Travel on the Cheap

I have to admit, it feels a bit odd for me to talk about this particular topic. Traveling has been a requirement and a privilege as part of my job at YouthWorks. I don't pay one dime out of my pocket for travel, but I've been entrusted with a budget to steward. I don't believe I'm the expert on cheap housing while traveling, but I can share some of what I have learned in my time as a traveling ministry guy.

I'm constantly aware of and honestly grateful for the funds that pay for my travel expenses. YouthWorks serves the church in many ways, but the main service we provide is short-term mission experiences. We receive a fee for our service, and those dollars are generated primarily through the tireless fundraising efforts of thousands of young people. Bake sales, car washes, support letters to grandparents—they all put money in my travel budget. Our organization is also indebted to hundreds of ministries and local congregations for partnering with us each summer, which keeps our monetary contributions relatively small, which in turn keeps our costs low, which allows for my non-support-raising job, let alone a healthy travel budget. If I'm careless and wasteful with those resources, I believe that sin would bring about a special kind of wrath from God. It's not my money; someone else worked for it and gifted it to a young person. I don't get to waste it.

I have very low comfort standards for where I sleep. Hardwood floors with a towel under my head work just fine. So crashing on an actual couch is a treat, especially if it's not in a youth room with who-knows-what on (and in) it.

My gender affords me the luxury to worry less about my safety as I travel. In general, women need to be a bit more selective regarding where they stay when traveling. It's just one of those things that makes it easier for me to travel cheap. Once I actually slept in a rental car in St. Louis. That was just dumb, but I don't know any woman (or many guys for that matter) who would feel safe doing that.

I utilize my network—even if a contact is one degree removed from me. Friends of friends can come in handy, but you also need a heavy amount of humility to ask folks to help you out. I find that nine times out of 10, even a last-minute ask will pay off. Most folks could care less if someone crashes on a couch or Hide-a-Bed. And if you do get in, act like your grandparents: Courtesy, gratitude, and cleanliness go a long way. Clean up after yourself; pull the sheets off the bed and fold 'em up, tidy up the room, clean out the bathtub, fold up your towels, and say thank you more than once in passing. The goal should be to leave the place like you weren't even there.

If you're a youth worker from a United Methodist church, for example, look up a few UMC churches in the town you're traveling to and ask the youth director if you can crash with her or him. Note: Don't ask someone of the opposite sex. It should go without saying, but being above reproach should be a high priority.

Shane Claiborne is my hero in regard to traveling cheap, and as a general principle, he'll never stay in a hotel. He was invited to speak at an event that was held at a sweet country club far away from everything, and instead he ended up sharing a room with a guy off-site at a Super 8. That was the only time I've heard of him breaking that "no hotels" rule, but he didn't have to pay for it.

Lastly, if you have to stay at a hotel, use Hotwire.com or Priceline.com or Kayak.com to book your room. And room with someone else (or a bunch of folks—especially at conferences). If you're staying a while, ask the hotel for a fridge and buy some of your food. Bagels and sandwiches are easy to make—and eat out for dinner. Saving money on two of three meals a day is huge. Or stay at a hotel that offers free breakfasts and chow down like all the people who lived through the Great Depression eating at buffets.

Stay at hotels with shuttles and skip renting a car. If they don't have shuttles, then get a round-trip deal from Super Shuttle or a similar outfit—way cheaper than a pair of one-way taxi rides. Or better yet, take public transportation. I like to fly to Midway Airport in Chicago (less crazy), then get a three-day $14 transit authority pass from a vending machine right next to the Orange Line. It's fun to take public transportation, and you save tons on rental, parking, and gas.

—*Eric Iverson*
YouthWorks!